CANCER'S SEEMING MADNESS

God's Story

By

Lloyd Austin Phillips

This book is a work of non-fiction.

ISBN: 0-7596-9414-1

Library of Congress Control Number: 2002093724

This book is printed on acid free paper.

Printed in the United States of America
Bloomington, IN

1stBooks - rev. 07/31/02

Dedicated
to
all who need God's help
in fanning the spark of life
after experiencing a crushing loss.

Foreword

It was the darkest time a parent could ever experience. The caller on the telephone asked that I sit down. "I have sad news," she shared in a whispered voice. "Your son, David, has been in an accident. He died earlier this afternoon..." Denial washed over me. I was attending an out of state seminar for judges. Three days earlier I had said goodbye at the airport to my wife, Karin, and our only child, David, who had just turned five years of age. David peered out the large glass windows of the airport as he excitedly told me about the airplanes landing and taking off. I shared my last words with him, "Take care of your mother. David, I ... love you."

Devastation. How could this happen? In my prayers just the evening before, I had thanked a loving God for a wonderful, caring wife and a healthy, extremely active, joyful and loving son who was the light of my life. My own father had died just three months earlier following a long illness and, in an instant, my son was now gone. Emptiness invaded my heart. It was the darkest of time.

When times are darkest, the light of the Lord's love illuminates our souls. I prayed for comfort and God's messenger, Pastor Lloyd Phillips, counseled me that God was shedding tears over the death of our son. He reminded me that God had sent His son Jesus so that my son and all who love the Lord will have everlasting life. Little would Pastor Lloyd know that years later his son, also named David, would die at an age far too young for us to understand. Yet, from that crushing loss, Pastor Lloyd Phillips has dedicated this book to "... all who need God's help in fanning the spark of life after experiencing a crushing loss." His eloquent, meaningful and poignant words provide comfort for others whose lives have been shattered by the toss of a loved one. Pastor Lloyd reminds us that God is faithful; God is forever and that nothing compares to the assurance we have of a glorious reunion with our loved ones... in the streaming sunlight of heaven.

John N. Fields
St. Joseph, Michigan

Introduction

Bonds between my son, David, and myself were strengthened as a result of the seeming madness of David's cancer. The story of how this played out is God's story. Of that, I am certain. It is a story that I believe will speak to all who struggle with spiritual issues in the context of the anomalies and crushing experiences of life. But, especially, it will speak to baby-boomers and their parents.

Before you read any further, I wish to say that in many ways David's presence is still a reality. Signs of that presence confirm, for me, that the veil between earth and heaven is very thin. A case in point occurred on the occasion of our son John's fiftieth birthday. John was named after the beloved disciple, John. In many ways for John's mother, Jean, and myself, our affection for John continues to be enhanced by his thoughtful, inclusive love. Attending his fiftieth birthday celebration was a joy-filled experience which gave us another opportunity to rejoice in having him as our son. Though his much beloved sister, Linda, could not attend, her talking gift created many laughs and was greatly appreciated by John. As for David, he was not present, or was he? Did David collaborate in providing a sign that I shall describe? I tell about it now, because visual phenomena related to David, who himself by trade was a sign-maker, is such an important part of God's story related in this book.

After John's "pig-picking" party was over, I engaged in another kind of pikin' called clean-up. The usual residue of an outdoor celebration needed attention; so I retrieved disposable items, including black balloons which are often used for fiftieth birthday celebrations as a jocular reminder of passage to a point where physical alacrity and mental acumen tend to diminish. As I neared the end of my labor, I noticed an inflated black balloon near some shrubbery in the neighbor's yard. Intending to retrieve the balloon, when I was about six feet from it, it started to rise from the ground, even though there was not the slightest breeze. I watched it until it became a tiny dot in the sky and then disappeared. Was this a sign of David's unseen presence at the party? I certainly would not rule out this possibility. At the very least, what to me was a mystery, became an assurance that there is a realm of joyous light and encompassing breath of the Spirit where the unseen presence of God and redeemed loved ones dwell. What a unique and powerful part of God's story this truth is!

Table Of Contents

Chapter 1

Looking At Promising Possibilities

David Lane Phillips was born during the Sunday School hour on October 4, 1953. Jean and I named David Lane after the great Old Testament king and my wife, Jean's, father. Sunday seemed a fitting time for the son of a preacher to be born. After his birth in Butterworth Hospital in Grand Rapids, I made my way to Oakdale Methodist Church with great joy and reported to my congregation gathered for worship on Evergreen Street the statistics of the newborn parsonage child. David brought into our family an evergreen kind of future filled with great promise. Only three years separated him from our first bundle of joy, John Lloyd. We saw the two brothers playing and growing together bringing into our lives excitement and new vistas along with the added responsibilities that attended the family scene.

David's interest and skills in art became apparent at an early age and blossomed during his teen years. This included, in addition to painting, thespian pursuits and music. These talents flourished in a young man who was a quick learner, curious, and gregarious. His sharp green eyes, winning smile, handsome features, and caring nature made him a person fun to be with.

What did the future hold for this son of promise? As David matured, he went down the road of independent thinking, decisive actions, and daring exploits. Place this person of energy and talent in the volatile period of the 60's and 70's, and what might you expect? The Viet Nam

1

war, the flower children, the Jesus people, the drug users were all a part of the explosive mix which was often lit by the flame of changing mores; corruption in high places; and a frantic devil-may-care attitude in the lives of those abused, discriminated against, and often despised by family, church, and society in general.

Many stories, some funny, others sad, and some pathetic could be told about the bumps in the road David surmounted, the curves he negotiated, and the wounds he received. Through it all, he emerged a young man of courage who really cared about the younger generation that would follow him. He developed a very successful sign business with a learning manual in one hand, and the "Wall Street Journal" in the other. He became an enemy of exploiters, and a friend of real people who learned from him and with him. In work, in recreation, in sun times and dark times, he gave to life his all, even at times in a reckless abandon that sapped away the vitals of his physical well-being.

The child of the 50's, and youth of the 60's and 70's became a young man of the 90's whose life hung in the balance because of the ravages of cancer. As the father of David and an ordained minister in the United Methodist Church, I was blessed by his love for me, but also troubled by the gnawing concern as to whether in all of the challenges and changes in his life's experiences David found strength in a core belief in a God who cared for him. Since I doubted such was the case, I prayed that the grace of Jesus Christ would draw David to the God of salvation. I prayed that there would be a movement of David's life toward God during the time that remained of the earthly calendar of his life. Was he not a child of promise - a recipient of God's covenant promise?

Chapter 2

Looking For The World Of God's Self-Revelation

Who is the God we talk about anyway? Some see God as a part of their wish fulfillment, thinking of Him as sort of a back up insurance if for some reason they can't make the mortgage payment when it is due. Others claim they feel the brush of angel's wings in the touchy, feely experiences of life that give them the assurance there is a God who cares for them. Many see themselves as a part of the whole universe which in its totality is deemed to be God. Others like my son, David, simply find joy in being with their friends with whom they experience the varied pleasures of life in which they sometimes overindulge. In this latter group, many are agnostic. Like David, they may allow for the possibility that there is a god. But if not, so what. Since they maintain that no one can prove God's existence, or non-existence, these agnostics pride themselves in being tolerant of those who give God various forms according to their needs and expectations.

So, for much of David's life the question of God's existence was of little concern. But when he learned of his terminal cancer, the God question occupied a place near center stage of his life. At that time he assured me that he would search after God, for what else in his life really mattered now. Knowing a God of faithful love, with confidence, I prayed and invited others to pray that David's life would be transformed by the miracle of God's redeeming love. That God is already at work through His Holy Spirit drawing persons to Himself even before we pray strengthens

3

the belief of the petitioner that the Christ who has begun His saving work will complete it to the glory of God who saves to the uttermost. When we pray according to His will, God hears and answers in keeping with His promise "Ask and it will be given you; seek and you will find; knock and the door will be opened to you." Mathew 7:7

Though God is a Spirit unseen, He is a sovereign God ever present and ready to bless the lives of those who seek Him and reach out for Him. The Apostle Paul bore witness to this truth when he said so eloquently in his address to the Greek philosophers on Mar's Hill in Athens, "The God who made the world and everything in it is the Lord of heaven and earth and does not live in temples built by hands. And he is not served by human hands, as if he needed anything, because he himself gives all men life and breath and everything else. From one man he made every nation of men, that they should inhabit the whole earth, and he determined the times set for them and the exact places where they should live. God did this so that men would seek him and perhaps reach out for him and find him, though he is not far from one of us, 'For in him we live and move and have our being.' As some of your own poets have said, 'We are his children.'" Acts 17:24-28.

In our spiritual exploration of God, whom Paul said "is not far from each one of us," we may find the parable of the philosopher Plato's cave to be a most helpful paradigm in learning what God is about in the process of making Himself and His purposes known to His children that they may follow a path of revelation that leads from the shadows of this life to the sunlight of his transforming presence in the life to come.

4

In the cave of my earthly existence through my tears and laughter God patiently made Himself known to me, especially during the last two weeks of my son, David's, life, but also during the space of time leading up to then, particularly following the diagnosis of his terminal cancer. The blessings that came to me and my family during the time of grasping and letting go were timeless and triumphant. So I share the highlights of our story, for I believe that in one form or another, at some point, this story God desires to be everyone's story.

Come with me into Plato's cave. In the cave Plato imagines people are chained and unable to move. They can direct their gaze only at one wall of the cave. Behind the prisoners is a fire on a raised path along which their wardens pass, casting shadows on the wall where the prisoner's eyes are fixed. The prisoners believe the shadows to be real figures. They watch the movements of the shadows, even predicting their changing positions. For the prisoners they are the real world. Then Plato imagines that for some reason one of the prisoners is able to turn around; and what he sees is a fire so dazzling that at first he cannot find his bearings. But after he becomes accustomed to his new situation, he acquires a knowledge different than the knowledge based only on moving shadows. What now? He is aware he cannot linger there for there is a fiery path before him which he must ascend. When he does, he finds himself facing the fullness of the brightness of the sun. At first the blinding experience of the fire is repeated, but with a much greater intensity. But by moving in the direction of the sun, the former prisoner of darkness finds final deliverance and great joy. His knowledge of a new found reality made possible by the sun is an experiential knowledge of goodness that transcends anything made possible by sense experience alone.

What Plato's character experienced while still in the cave was real, but only partial. And whereas he entered a new realm of knowledge and experience when he left the cave, even in that new realm total reality remained to some degree veiled by the very sun of transcendent goodness that made possible his new found joy, freedom and knowledge of the good. In Christian thought Plato's supreme form which he calls the good is easily identified with God. The good becomes the essence of God's self-revelation which is seen as an ever expanding reality now and in the world(s) to come.

The story of David's journey leading up to and including his blessed spiritual transformation left its mark on his family, because we all have had our beginning in the natural, shadowy world which is also God's world. As in the parable of Plato's cave, this world in which we are at times prisoners is in a shadowy sense a manifestation of this world, or worlds which transcend it, and of the God who created it all. Later on I'll expand on this thought in what I have to say about the Christian concept of providence.

Chapter 3

Looking at Lane Signs

As we have noted in the parable of Plato's cave, the shadows were signs of a transcendent ideal. David established a company headquartered in London, KY, which he named Lane Signs, Lane being his maternal grandfather's and his middle name. In addition to hand painted signs, he did truck lettering, murals and graphics, billboards, plastic and metal letters, neon signs and electrical signage. So somewhat like the shadows in Plato's cave, materially speaking, Lane Signs pointed to realities of interest to those with a need for information and/or direction.

David's life also consisted of spiritual signs that pointed to perfect, ideal values revealed by the God we know in Jesus Christ. This same Jesus who reveals God can be seen in every human being, however blurred and imperfect His image may be. As we are reminded in Matthew 25, Jesus is seen in persons who are hungry, thirsty, strangers, naked, prisoners, and the sick - all the needy, forgotten and despised to whom we are called to relate in love.

In Basel, Switzerland, there is a sculpture on the front wall of St. Martin's Church depicting Martin of Tours, a Roman soldier who was a Christian. It seems that on a cold winter day when Martin was entering a city, he was stopped by a beggar asking for alms. The story goes that having no money, Martin took off his coat, cut it in two and gave half to the beggar. In a dream that night, Martin was in heaven where he saw Jesus wearing half of a Roman soldier's coat. When an angel asked Him,

"Master, why are you wearing that battered old cloak?", Jesus answered, "My servant Martin gave it to me." We, too, meet Jesus when in love we reach out to help the needy.

In the following eulogy I wrote which was read in a very moving way by his brother, John, at David's Memorial Service, Lane's spiritual signs were celebrated. Take note of the ways in which Jesus was seen in David in the eulogy that was given on July 23, 1997, at David's Memorial Service held in St. William's Church, London, KY.

Eulogy

Recently, on the 4th of July, we celebrated our nation's birthday.

In doing so, we were once again reminded by the Declaration of Independence that "all men are endowed by their Creator with certain unalienable rights, that among them are life, liberty and the pursuit of happiness." In the original Declaration, the words creator, rights, life, liberty and happiness are all capitalized, emphasizing the faith of our forefathers in God, and their belief that God intended that all persons should be able to enjoy the blessings of freedom. In that same spirit my son, David, wrote the following in a letter to the press just prior to the appearance of members of the Ku Klux Klan in downtown London: "Being the son of a Methodist minister, I have seen the many different effects that Christianity can have on people, and have experienced what I perceive to be true Christian love. Unselfishness, humility, moderation, generosity, sympathy and tolerance have all been a part of this love. I have seen people work together towards positive, meaningful goals, helping those less fortunate, without thought of reward. There are truly many beautiful aspects of the human spirit that I am confident I would never have experienced without my exposure to religion.

Unfortunately, I have also met some abusers of the faith who use religion as a self-serving crutch to abuse others while attaining their own selfish goals and ideals. The most dangerous abusers of the faith are those who do not know who they are; who really believe that what they are doing draws strength from the Christian religion. Their abuse is based on ignorance, on their fears of what they do not understand. They have no tolerance, no compassion, or love. The hatred and the suspicion that they attempt to spread is the antithesis of Christian love, the opposite message that Christ came to preach."

After offering a suggestion of how a protest might be made, David concluded his remarks concerning a response to the K.K.K. by saying, "All citizens should, in whatever form, make their feelings known. Whatever form the protest takes, it needs to take place. Draw out the display of darkness with one of light."

Those whose lives were touched by David knew him to be a loving, kind and compassionate person. His love was not mere sentiment. It took the form of an active, courageous stand for justice. He championed the cause of those unjustly oppressed. David would agree with John F. Kennedy who said, "There are risks and costs to a program of action. But they are far less than the long-range risks and costs of comfortable inaction."

David's love was not only expressed in the public square, but also in the whole realm of nature which even included the python. But he supremely loved in that area of life where love is most severely tested, namely, in the family. He bequeathed to family members love in many forms. Oh, sure, there were times when he tried the patience of his wife, disappointed his parents, and created virtual chaos in his sibling relationships; but in the end, his love prevailed.

One day the writer Elizabeth Barrett Browning went to the side of her poet husband, Robert Browning, who had fallen asleep at his desk while working on his poetry, and she wrote this note for him to see: "My dearest Robert, my whole world, my whole life, my whole future has been different since that day I first felt thy footsteps walk across my soul."Ask David's wife, Bernadette, about David's footsteps across her soul that brought gifts of love into her life.

Ask David's mother, Jean, and father, Lloyd, how David taught them to joyfully and honestly express the love one feels for those near and dear. In humility and gratitude they will tell you how in the early 70's David helped them learn the truth embedded in this quotation from Gibran's The Prophet: "Your children are not your children. They are the sons and daughters of Life's longing for itself. They come through you but not from you. And though they are with you, yet they belong not to you. You may give them your love but not your thoughts. For they have their own thoughts. You may house their bodies, but not their souls. For their souls dwell in the house of tomorrow which you cannot visit, not even in your dreams. You may strive to be like them, but seek not to make them like you. For life goes not backward nor tarries with yesterday."

In Galatians 5:22, the Apostle Paul wrote: "But the fruit of the Spirit is love." Then the apostle followed with words that describe the characteristics and working of love. The first word so used was joy. True joy is experienced when we share love with those we care about.

The story is told of a policeman who saw a penguin in the street;so he stopped his squad car and picked it up to take it to the zoo. But meantime he got an emergency call which interrupted his intention. Seeing his street-wise friend, Stosh, he said to him, "Do you mind taking this penguin to the zoo?" Stosh replied, "Glad to."The next day when he saw Stosh and the penguin downtown, the policeman said to Stosh, "I thought I told you to take the penguin to the zoo." Stosh replied, "I did, but I had so much fun I thought I would take him to the ball game today."

After I told David that story, he groaned, as you might well imagine. Why then do I tell it again to you? I tell it to say this: David took many penguins to zoos and ball games. He enjoyed helping others have fun when he acted a part in a children's play; cooked a gourmet meal; took friends on a boat ride; threw a party; or played with his grandson, Brandon. David related to his sons, Frank and Paul, in playful and positive ways; made so many days special for his beloved Bernadette, whom he bragged about and encouraged in her endeavors; visited parents, Jean and Lloyd, in Michigan and showered them with surprises in thoughtful, affirmative and loving ways; and, yes, was proud to be a brother to Linda and John whom he loved with genuine affection.

Perhaps you would like to share your joy by telling us something you remember about David. Many stories could be told indicating how David was daring, innovative, creative and passionate about life. His life was laced with humor and serious endeavor, and much in-between. Celebrate his life now by sharing your remembrance of David.

Respondents:

The responses of two persons to the invitation to share were very moving. One was a Christian young man who was a stranger to the thespian group that put on plays for children in two Kentucky counties. David took him under his wing and made him feel very welcomed in the group. This young man stated that after participating with David in a particular play, he knew that his new found friend was a very special person. He related that David said to him, after a scene in that play, "Remember me." These words which seemed to say, "I cherish your friendship, too," cemented their friendship.

The other respondent was the altar girl who said that though she did not know David, she felt blessed being present for the memorial celebration of David's life, which for her was a "very moving experience."

Chapter 4

Looking At The "D" Word

It was in April of 1997 that Jean and I learned that David had been diagnosed as having cancer. The cancer, we were told, was found in the lung and brain areas of his anatomy. We did not know whether the spread of the dread disease was more extensive than original tests indicated. We got word of the alarming news to his sister, Linda, and also to his brother, John, who was stationed with the Army in Korea.

The thought did not occur to us that David's time with us would be a brief three months ending with the Memorial Celebration when the eulogy included in the previous chapter was given. Surely, David, a vibrant young man, would not succumb. Despite the shock to us, we were not ready to acknowledge the "D" word, death, would soon strike down a member of our family. After all, we could rely on the benefits of medical science and prayer. And radium treatments would soon begin.

Oh, sure, we were deeply concerned about what could be a painful and prolonged struggle. But David was a survivor. Then one day when I called David, he told me that he was trying to put up a hammock where he could relax and enjoy the nice weather they were having. Apparently, what normally would have been a snap for him to accomplish was now a real chore. Then he said something which for me was very chilling. He said to me, "I know I am dying." I tried to muster a response that might be an attempt to implant encouragement, but somehow it didn't work. The awkward void was filled by a diversionary question he directed to me,

13

"How is your book coming?" He was genuinely interested, because he had asked the question before and knew the project must be about completed. But this time he asked the question to put me at ease. I told him that as soon as the publishing house sent me the copies of my finished book, I would see that he got one. He was pleased to hear this. Ironically, the book was about end times. As he was approaching what he deemed to be his earthly end time, he was interested to see what I had to say in the book I authored, <u>Fire From The Sky</u>, which contains twenty essays on the Biblical book of <u>Revelation</u>.

David had seemed so alone when I talked to him on the phone. In a physical sense he was temporarily alone, because Bernadette had not returned from work. But he was psychologically alone, too. No one could die for him. He saw his situation as terminal, even before others used the term. Like when as a little boy he played by himself in his play pen for hours, he now, again, found himself alone in a world that was uniquely his. But this new world was collapsing around him. This was a young man who as a boy was not properly strapped in a carnival ride that whirled him around, but then he survived. This was the same young man who as a boy climbed a rickety ladder of a fire watcher's tower on a mountain top in Maine, but then he survived.

Later I learned that David had befriended a neighbor who had terminal cancer. He spoke words of encouragement to him; wrote him a letter that gave him hope (so the man told me); and made him a sign that he had requested without charging him. Now that he shared the same fate as his neighbor - would friends be present for David to help him through his wrenching experience?

In another call to David, he told me he had climbed down a very steep hill to see how the Brandywine tomato plants he had planted were coming. He was glad that he made it back up the hill. As I learned more about my son's condition, I became aware that life for him was spiraling out of control. He was unable to do simple math which was a part of his bookkeeping related to his sign work. This was frustrating for a person with a keen intellect who learned so quickly, and absorbed abstract ideas so easily. I learned that in the recent past, on more than one occasion when he knew he was blacking out, that he had to pull over the vehicle he was driving to the side of the road. His brain tumor condition spelled havoc. Radium treatment had begun.

Did David's friends offer support by their presence, practical deeds, and conversations about past experiences that had linked their lives in so many wonderful ways? Yes, they did. Wife, Bernadette; sons, Paul and Frank; members of Bernadette's family, including her saintly mother; plus siblings Linda and John; many working and recreational companions; and even past acquaintances, including some who barely knew David, touched his life in countless ways as much as human beings can. His mother and father spent many difficult, but very meaningful days and nights by David's side. The young man born in Michigan who was given the honorary title of "Kentucky Colonel" because of his community service, particularly in connection with London's Annual Chicken Festival, was not forgotten.

David was at ease with persons from many ethnic backgrounds whom he counted friends. Among these were Jewish bakery owners from New York City, Mexicans, Italians, African Americans, to name a few.

15

Included among his friends were persons of different sexual orientations, and those of differing economic, cultural, and religious and non-religious backgrounds.

My son returned to Michigan to visit his mother and myself every so often. He would sometimes bring a gift of some kind, whether it was a painting, or berries and/or vegetables that he picked or grew. Most of all he brought himself and shared generously of his time and thoughts. One time he strung out a fishing line that was tangled by walking with it partially around our pond so that he could straighten it out for further use. On another occasion he brought a laminated copy of a newspaper article he had written concerning the perfidy of the Ku Klux Klan, and how he believed religious persons should respond concerning their planned visit to Main Street, London, KY. He titled his letter to the editor, "Group of Intellectual Mutants Plan to March." One can see why we cherished David not only as a son, but also as a friend and an astute and caring person.

He often expressed his loving friendship with cards we received on special occasions. I have before me, as I write, two cards that illustrate my point. On the inside of the birthday card it reads, "Have a wonderful day - It's your day to be King!" There is an artistic painting of a lion, the king of the beasts, on the front of the card. After the card's words I quoted which were on the inside, he wrote, "And every other day, too. Thank you for all you have done for me..(even the ears)." He was referring to my large ears. Then he signed the card, "Best wishes always. Love, David." Inside the 1994 Father's Day card, it reads, "Happy Father's Day. You are and you will always be the most important part of all the dreams, the hopes and plans that are closest to my heart!" He then adds in his own words,

"Thanks so much for all you have given and continue to give. I am blessed with the most beautiful father in the world. All my Love, David."

Now you know why for Jean and myself the "D" word was so disconcerting and unwelcome when first we heard David use it as he spoke of the prospect he faced. While we still miss David's physical presence, and continue to shed tears of loving remembrance, you'll see as the story of our relationship with him during his last days on earth unfolds that the "D" word takes on a new and glorious significance. How so? Because we now see the awesome "D" as a prelude pointing to a new and blessed reality of triumphant grace. The friendship of which I write now centers for our family in a much deeper sense in the God we know in Jesus Christ.

In the Christian doctrine of the incarnation, God becoming flesh in Jesus Christ, we see a God who draws us to Himself in friendship. This God offers us perfect beatitude, the foretaste of which may be known in this life. Jesus as a man has made this friendship possible. As God, He has sealed that friendship. Jesus satisfies the need for a human God and a Divine human being in His united two natures.

By our wills and intellects we may seek to apprehend God more fully, whereas, the God-man, Jesus, from the start of His earthly journey had a direct apprehension of God. Therefore, in all cultural and social circumstances He revealed in His teaching and by His deeds, not only the divine will for human beings, but also revealed in Himself through His crucifixion and resurrection the means of human salvation. And so Jesus became the death of death. To become such by laying down His life for us, He revealed the length, breadth, depth and height of God's love. So the

Apostle John wrote as recorded in John 15:13, "Greater love has no man than this, that one lay down his life for his friends." Therefore, death, as Paul wrote, has lost its "sting" and its "victory".

1 Corinthians 15:55.

Chapter 5

Looking At Body And Blood

Though we knew that David had cancer in his lungs and brain, we didn't know how pervasive it was in his body, nor what his prognosis would be. So he entered a Lexington, KY, hospital to learn about treatment options based on the nature of his condition, and the possible bearing this would have on his future. David and his body and blood family would be confronted with the issue of life and death.

It was a time of apprehension, but also joyful interchange. David did not suffer from physical pain then, nor later, because the tumor growth in his brain cut off the messages of pain - so we were told by those medically trained to understand such things. David and Linda enjoyed each other's company often filling his room with laughter as they recalled their days growing up together. They were even permitted to leave the hospital to shop for treats at a nearby store. Or did they just slip out?

A minister from Granger, Indiana, called ahead to arrange for Jean and myself gratis lodging adjacent to the hospital. The minister also contacted the hospital chaplain whose comforting presence was welcomed by David. Missing from our family group was John, who though he arranged to return from Korea, as yet had not returned to the States.

I felt led of the Lord to offer communion to family members willing to participate. On the spur of the moment I secured communion elements from the hospital and got family members together in David's room. Absent was David's wife, Bernadette, who was in the chapel on another

19

floor in the hospital. Though she likely would have participated had she been in the area, we conjectured that she might be returning to David's room before communion was celebrated and join us there. After discussing the matter with David and other family members, we decided not to look for her realizing how much comfort she received and gave others during her chapel visits.

What I did not know was whether David would be willing to receive communion. I knew that he would not receive communion just out of deference to me. He was not one to play games. But I thought he might decide in his own mind to do so as a symbol of our spiritual oneness as a family. That he did, despite any theological reservations he may have had.

The Scripture that I read before communion was First John 4:7-12. Verse 7 reads, "Beloved, let us love one another; for love is of God, and he who loves is born of God and knows God." In my comments on the verse I shared with those about to take communion the essence of what Greek scholar, J. B. Phillips, wrote on page 67 in his book Ring of Truth concerning this verse: "But if it is true, as John declares, that 'God is love,' it would make sense that any action that sprang from love had its origin in God. It would also mean that those who did give themselves in love to others did in fact 'know God,' however loudly they might protest their agnosticism." Verse 9 and 10 of First John refer to the manifestation of God's love in the sacrifice of His Son for our sins. David had no problem with this possibly being a manifestation of God's love, but wondered about what seemed to be an inherent exclusiveness related to Jesus' sacrifice. I responded that I was concerned about the claim of some who believe that a "correct" understanding of a particular doctrine is

20

necessary, in this case a knowledge of a "correct" understanding of the atonement, or else those who don't have it will be excluded from "life" made possible by Jesus, God's love gift. But then I went on to say that God's inclusiveness is guaranteed by the extraordinary, astonishing claim that John, the beloved disciple, makes in verse 12: "No man has ever seen God; but if we love one another, God abides in us and his love is perfected in us." I then went on to point out that the supreme love inherent in Jesus' sacrifice teaches us the nature of God's ever faithful love. I emphasized that God's faithful love in conjunction with the sacrifice of Jesus made it possible for us to love one another with the same love wherewith we have been loved in Jesus.

Following this discussion, I cited examples of how David made known God's love by his concern about issues of peace, justice and equality, and by his involvement in troubles and burdens of others. I went on to say that God's love for him was very special, especially at that very time of crisis in his life and ours. I explained that by taking communion together we would be expressing our love for God and one another, and would be acknowledging His love for us, especially in the sacrifice of His Son. Reservations still? Perhaps, but we all truly received communion in the wonder of love. For me, and I believe for others in David's hospital room that day, His Body and Blood were real.

What about David's body and blood? The next day David and all of us gathered in a room to learn what a doctor highly skilled in oncology had to tell us as a result of David's tests. He told us that the spread of cancer in David's body was very extensive. Not only was it present in his brain and lungs, but also in his pancreas. The tenseness present when we entered this room increased. Questions concerning treatment and likely length of life were answered. Chemotherapy would be available, but no treatment would cure - only forestall death. As to span of life? We were told David would likely only have 9 - 12 months.

David's response was immediate and decisive. He said he was interested in quality of life, so would not opt for chemo treatments. When shock subsided, emotions were rampant. Feelings of sympathy and anger were evident among family members which gave rise to words ranging from measured advice to sharp retorts.

Not long after the thud of blasted hopes, family members prepared to leave for their respective homes. In the days ahead as we lived beneath dark clouds of imminent death, many thoughts and memories filled our days.

David's days were filled with frustration. His ability to carry on his sign work was virtually nonexistent. He did try to tie up loose ends related to some of his work, but this only contributed to further stress. His life was spiced by friends who still stopped by to chat with him and enjoy a smoke and can of beer. These were important intervening spaces of time that brought him a modicum of relief, but increased the distress of some who were aware of the nicotine curse that robbed David of the sweetness of life itself.

David found strength during his last days from memories of the sweetness of life he had known and was able to describe so well. Of this I am certain. Anyone in touch with the charm and beauty of life as much as David was had a memory account he could draw upon. Many such memories were related to the life he shared with Bernadette and sons, Paul and Frank, in the "tranquil backroads of southern Kentucky." Read, with delight, one such memory which he wrote about in March of 1996:

Hillbilly Heaven

I still enjoy fond and vivid memories of the first journey that "Mom & Dad" Dionisio made to visit our family in the backwoods of Kentucky. One of the biggest factors that made this trip so memorable to me was the culture shock experienced not only by Mom and Dad, but also by our neighbors.

They made this journey by automobile, coming from the noisy and congested streets of the southern Bronx, to the twisting yet tranquil backroads of southern Kentucky. It was these twisting roads which led to their first experience with culture shock. Actually, I suppose that the term "topography shock" would be more accurate.

Upon this night time arrival, Mom and Dad related to us their treacherous journey on the highway leading to our humble little shack; a mountainous and winding road, which Tony, in particular seemed to believe, was about to fall down the mountainside at any moment, taking the Plymouth Valiant with it. (As well as the stream of resident drivers behind them who were wondering, no doubt, "where in the hell did these New York Yankees come from?")

I believe that the environment seemed a little less dangerous after a good night's sleep. As daylight bathed our surroundings, the mountains on all sides changed from threatening to sheltering, and both Tony and Beatrice could better understand what had drawn their youngest daughter to live in such a place. I believe that "Mother MacCree" to borrow one of

23

Bernadette's terms of endearment, understood the best. She seemed to me to be totally in her element, washing clothes on a scrubboard, drawing water by hand from the well, gathering fresh eggs and even visiting our two-seater outhouse, in lieu of the "5-gallon flush". She seemed at peace which was heartwarming to watch.

Not to imply that Tony was unappreciative of our situation by any means. As a true lover of nature and animals, he too experienced his peace. Even after our "killer" rooster attacked him and sent him sprawling to the ground, to be rescued by Frank, he seemed to be content in these foreign surroundings. However, I still don't think that he exactly understood why we did not have a flush toilet.

Among all the pleasant memories of this first visit, there is one in particular that for some reason is etched in my memory. It was the meeting of two cultures, and although each of the participants were American citizens, living 800 miles apart, it seemed to be an alien affair.

There was a family living across the road named the Davidsons. Tyree and Sally. They had three sons, and were about the same age as mom and dad. Their eldest son, Ronald, had already fled the nest, married and fathered a daughter whom they named Freddy-Gal; I believe they were expecting a boy. Clinton, the middle boy, was around sixteen years old and never "quite right". He was presumed to be retarded. Tyree once told me that when they sent Clinton to school for the first few days, he would leave at the earliest opportunity and walk home. So they just decided to quit sending him. Otis, the youngest son, was about the same age as Frank and Paul, and they played together nearly every day.

Anyway, the moment that I remember most was when the Dionisios met the Davidsons. As in all Appalachian familial encounters, the males dominated the conversation. So here's the picture: Tyree, with his profound Kentucky accent, a man who laughs a toothless laugh as often as he speaks and who often would let out a whooping sound like Ernest T. Bass on "The Andy Griffith Show", attempting conversation with a man who has a profound Italian/New York accent and uses words and terms that Tyree doesn't even understand. Soon, Beatrice and Sally join in the fray and all are cackling away happily with each other. The amazing thing to me was that, although each participant probably understood about half of what the other was saying, there was communication taking place. They were having a true conversation even though they weren't understanding each other verbally! Good feelings flowed back and forth, to be felt by all involved. It was wonderful!

So there you have it; my little moment. Who knows why certain things stick with you? Of course, it was only one moment of the many I have shared with my "other parents". And although one of them has since relocated, the memories will always remain.

To you, Mom, thank you for all the warm memories you have given me as well as those to come. Happy 79th Birthday!

I love you,

David-in-Law

David's mother-in-law, Beatrice, did bring him more "warm memories" after those described so poignantly in "Hillbilly Heaven". But more than memories are present in the writing. David's love of people is highlighted as well.

After we learned of David's prognosis in the Lexington, KY, hospital, would he also remember the Body and Blood of Lexington that drew us close to God and one another in the bonds of love? Did an even more blessed heaven lie in his future?

Chapter 6

Looking At A Pool Table

By now our family knew that unless God intervened in some miraculous way, David's days remaining would be not only few but likely would also be characterized by mercurial feelings followed by unpredictable reactions.

David's friends knowing he liked to play pool bought him a good pool table that fit perfectly on his patio. By now David was virtually bald due to radium therapy, but his physical prowess allowed him to still play a fairly mean game of pool.

The thoughtful gift was not only enjoyed by David, but also by his friends and family. Love, laughter, and friendly competition around the table helped ease the pain of facing more days of deteriorating health, and actually brought joy for moments that otherwise would have been bleak.

Symbolically, I suppose the table in this setting represented the ways one seeks to cope with the challenges, dangers, and setbacks of life. When the caroms of life put us behind the eight ball, how may we rebound and make the most of the situation? What cue sticks do we rely upon to hit the balls we want to fall into the pockets of life?

Up until now, I haven't mentioned how Jean and I were able to cope. The cue sticks of love, prayer and God's faithfulness became increasingly important to us. Following the prognosis, we increased our contacts with David and Bernadette through telephone calls, writings and visits. Not only were they continually in our prayers, but also remembered on many

27

prayer chains. We knew that being an overcomer required faithfulness. But now as never before that virtue was being tested.

At the heart of faithfulness in the context of one's relationship to God is joyful obedience. Under the stress of testing related to the dying of a loved one, joyful obedience does not come naturally. But God never requires anything of us apart from His willingness to give us enabling grace. His enablement came when I was asked to preach on April 27, 1997. I did so based on a portion of <u>Revelation</u> contained in Chapter 2, Verses 8-11 which includes these words, "Be faithful, even to the point of death, and I will give you the crown of life." In my time of mourning, these comforting words of Holy Writ motivated me to obey God's call to joyfully serve.

There were two main points in my sermon. They were number one: The Key To Overcoming Is Faithfulness, and the second point was: Faithfulness Is The Antidote For Fear. Included in the sermon was a quote from Evelyn Underhill who has written with excellent insight on the contemplative life. The quote was: "A Christian should be like a sheep dog. When the shepherd wants him to do something, he lies down at his feet, looks intently into the shepherd's eyes, and listens without budging until he has understood the mind of his master. Then he jumps to his feet and runs to do it. And the third characteristic which is no less important: at no moment does the dog stop wagging its tail."

Late in April and early in May, David seemed to have a new spurt of energy. John who had been on duty in Korea had received permission to come home early from his army assignment in that country so that he could see David. Weather-wise the timing was also perfect for John to do

28

things with his sibling whom he fondly referred to as "my little brother". John, too, found the pool table to be a new friend. But more importantly, the friendship of two brothers at this crucial moment in their lives was beautiful to behold. So I was told by one of David's best friends. Small talk was now big talk. Their precious time together was golden. In a sense it was a rekindling of friendship, for their respective interests and duties had given little opportunity for them to occupy common ground. Special occasions had brought them together for brief periods, but one on one times had been too infrequent. But now the pool table was a symbol of a true love that came alive. Leisurely times on the beautiful lake at the bottom of the hill where David's home was located was the order of the day. David's role was now captain of the boat that in the beautiful month of May carried John and members of David's immediate Kentucky family to the familiar inlets where David fished and spent time with family and friends on lazy Sunday afternoons. For use on that same lake David built a pontoon boat which he later sold. With the help of friends he also built a dock from which now he and John embarked.

Jean and I were not a part of the halcyon days our two sons enjoyed, but we were so grateful that they were together at a time when they experienced great camaraderie mixed with the knowledge that this would likely be one of the last times their paths would cross in this life. For John the good memories of the time spent together are lasting, and for Jean and myself the pictures that captured some of their high moments are a treasure.

Had all the balls on the pool table fallen in the right pockets? The answer may depend on the day the question is asked. By faith my answer is, "Yes." Because I believe on the basis of God's Word that eternity will provide a final reassuring answer, I continue David's story by looking back at his baptism.

Chapter 7

Looking at Water

Under the covenant that God made with Abraham, during the Old Testament period the circumcision of males when they were eight days old was a sign of God's covenant with Abraham and his physical and spiritual offspring, Genesis 17:11-12. God promised that He would be faithful to His "covenant of love to a thousand generations." Deuteronomy 7:9. Under the new covenant, the water of baptism, applicable to both male and female who are one in Christ, described as "circumcision made without hands" in Colossians 2:11-12, replaced physical circumcision as a sign and seal of the covenant. Now in effect the new covenant is ratified in the lives of those baptized; for their baptism symbolizes their relationship to the crucified and risen Christ, Romans 6:4.

In Acts we learn that adult believers were baptized as a sign and seal of their commitment to Christ. Furthermore, this same sign and seal was given to members of their households at the time of their baptism, Acts 16:15,33. This practice of having their children baptized was in keeping with what Peter admonished in Acts 2:38-39 where he associates forgiveness and the gift of the Holy Spirit not only with adult baptism, but also with the baptism of their children. So we see from the teaching of the New Testament that baptism of both adults and their children is a sign and seal of God's covenant faithfulness in Jesus Christ.

Despite the efficacy of baptism for both adults and children as a sign and seal of promised salvation as it relates to God's covenant, it must be emphasized that baptism is not a rite that creates regeneration, which is spiritual new birth. The Apostle Peter declares in I Peter 3:21 that baptism does not automatically insure salvation in a mechanical way as in the cleansing that occurs when one's body is washed. But rather, baptism which replaced circumcision as a faith rite, therefore like circumcision is a sign and seal of justification by faith, Romans 4:11. For the believing adult, baptism looks back on the justification that has already occurred through faith. For the children, baptism looks forward to the time when the justifying faith known by their parents will also be theirs when by faith they receive the promised gift of salvation. Salvation for the child is like a blank check given that must be filled out. The parent's role in teaching the faith by word and deed is vital. But even if the parents fail to teach, or their children rebel, God's promises given to their children at baptism remain an open door into the community of faith. So baptism for the child is a very important purveyor and means of grace. It is a purveyor when through the Holy Spirit's prompting the promises of Acts 2:38-39 are claimed on behalf of the child. Mark 2:5, 10-12 reminds us that Jesus honors the faith of believers on behalf of those in need of healing and salvation!

When Jean and I had our son, David, baptized as an infant, we knew that the water of baptism was grace-filled water. Knowing that salvation is truly and solely a gift of God's grace, we were grateful that grace was given to David through baptism. His spiritual journey had begun. We covenanted with God to be obedient so that we might claim the promise of Proverbs 22:6: "Train a child in the way he should go, and when he is old he will not turn from it."

Shortly before David was born, I wrote a paper for my seminary theology class in answer to the question we were given by our professor: "What did God promise John, an individual son of believing parents, when he was baptized Sunday?" The question seemed pertinent, because before I received the assignment our older son John had been baptized. After my seminary assignment was completed, we anticipated that if God blessed us with the birth of another child that he or she would also receive the covenant promises associated with baptism. Furthermore, we were aware of our privilege and responsibility to teach as indicated in my paper's concluding words: "Even before John was born, when his parents professed Christ and became members of the visible church, they covenanted for him as well as themselves. Because they understood the implications then, in confident faith they now assume in regards to John the responsibility contained in the injunction found in Ephesians 6:4, 'Bring them up in the nurture and admonition of the Lord.'"

When David became an adult, it was evident that he had not forsaken many of the values he had learned as a child. But the question with which Jean and I wrestled was what about his faith? Who or what was his God? Had this boy who sang in the Cherub Choir when he was young, and attended Sunday School, and participated in youth groups as he grew older, forsaken his faith? His love of people, respect for life in general, and sense of justice were evident to all who knew him. His love for us was never an issue. With joy we honored him as a son and were proud of him. And yet, he claimed to be an agnostic. But he never rejected Jesus, or ridiculed our faith. He had built many beautiful relationships. Many parents lauded him for the positive influence he had on their children whom he loved. Through dramatic roles he taught them many <u>basic</u> lessons that would build character. Especially in Laurel and Rockcastle Counties in Kentucky, he survives through the good will and friendships that are still cherished by those who knew him. In many respects he built well and on solid ground. And yet certain things about his lifestyle would lead some to question whether, to use the Apostle Paul's language, he had built on a foundation "using gold, silver, costly stones, wood, hay or straw." After speaking of these possibilities, Paul said as recorded in I Corinthians the third chapter and verses fourteen and fifteen, "If what he has built survives, he will receive his reward. If it is burned up, he will suffer loss; he himself will be saved, but only as one escaping through the flames."

I write not to enshrine David as a saint, nor do I who have been often a weak follower of my Lord claim to be his judge. I believe though that for the most part he used good building materials, and despite his claim to be an agnostic, I believe he knew the God of creation. At his Memorial Service, Father Stern spoke of his qualities that were akin to St. Francis of Assisi. With this I would agree. But before he died, my prayer was that he would also come to know and love the God of redemption in Jesus Christ. I didn't expect stigmata would appear on his body, but my deepest desire was that he would experience in a personal and intimate way the love of God who cared for him so much that he gave His Son as a sacrifice for his sins. Then his entrance into the eternal kingdom would not be "as one escaping through the flames", but as a child of God redeemed by Jesus Christ and filled with peace and joy.

Eighteen years before David died, I preached a sermon entitled, "Grace-Filled Water." At one point in the sermon alluding to Romans 5:6,8, I said, "For while we were yet sinners, Christ died for us, the godly for the ungodly. This is the basis for the transformation of sinners into saints. For many of us that transformation began at the time of baptism, for the waters of baptism beyond all seeing become grace-filled waters." These would become prophetic words for what would take place in David's life. So in a very profound way the Lord affirmed through my lips how God's saving work would transform David's life.

The Lord's transforming presence in David's inner being during his final days of terminal illness <u>became</u> for Jean and myself a source of sustaining comfort. We witnessed the truth of Isaiah's words written in Isaiah 43:19a, "See, I am doing a new thing!" Through the Holy Spirit's work the affirmation came alive. A pastor asked me, "What verses in the Bible give you hope and strength in connection with David's situation?" I told him that I held on to the promises associated with baptism in Acts 2:38-39. Then I said, "I have peace, great peace, that all will be well with David." The Holy Spirit had borne witness with my spirit concerning the truth of Isaiah's words, "See, I am doing a new thing!"

With a renewed faith, we continued to claim for David the promises of Acts 2:38-39. His water baptism pointed to the baptism of the Holy Spirit that he would receive. It was then that the Holy Spirit would bear witness with David's spirit that because he trusted in Jesus who died for him, he would live eternally with the Lord. The peace of God that he would receive by grace through faith would make it possible for him to enter triumphantly into the Kingdom of eternal light. This fulfillment of God's promises Jean and I knew would bring us great joy, even during the time of our mourning.

Chapter 8

Looking At David's Wonderful
Words Of Love and Life

David's search for God during the trying days of his terminal illness was a sign of God's love for him, confirming the words of I John 4:19, "We love because he first loved us." Our desire to know our Creator and Redeemer is sparked by His love for us made known in Jesus Christ. David's written and spoken words which expressed his love for family and his quest for truth, even in the context of his anguish, revealed that God through Jesus Christ chose to give him spiritual birth "through the word of truth" that he might become an heir "having the hope of eternal life." These quotations are from James 1:18 and Titus 3:7. As Jean and I became aware of what was taking place in David's life, the words of Philip P. Bliss' hymn "Wonderful Words of Life" - especially the second stanza took on new meaning: "Christ, the blessed one, gives to all wonderful words of life: sinner, list to the loving call, wonderful words of life; all so freely given, wooing us to heaven. Beautiful words, wonderful words, wonderful words of life."

Often times Jean in writing to David would quote hymns, such as the one cited. In this way God's faithful love for David was expressed through the love of his mother. The last Mother's Day card in which David had an opportunity in writing to acknowledge their mutual love was on May 11, 1997. He wrote:

"Dear Mother,

This Mother's Day holds an extra special meaning for me -
I'm sure you know what I mean. I couldn't ask for one bit more
than you have given me for you are the finest.
None of us knows what the future holds in store for us, but
there is one thing of which I am sure. There is no greater love than
what we have shared and hopefully will continue to share for many
years to come.
I love you for now and for eternity.

Your son,
David"

On May 10, we had received a call that his condition had deteriorated considerably. He had written on the Mother's Day card that he hoped to share his love with his mother for many years. But he had also written about the uncertainty of the future. Even so, he affirmed that he would love his mother for eternity. How blessed that this faith was embedded in his mind.

Shortly after receiving the telephone call, we went to Banner Book store in St. Joseph, MI, where we were involved in a book signing for <u>Fire From The Sky</u>. While there, a friend gave to us a message from her daughter which read, "Trust, Believe, Expect a Miracle." This message prompted by David's illness was welcomed. The miracle was already at work in David who had written concerning "love...for eternity."

As soon as we could, we made our way to London, Kentucky. Our vivacious and loving daughter, Linda, went with us. In London in celebration of Mother's Day, we went to a Chinese restaurant. We were somewhat surprised after receiving the telephone call that David was exuberant about the plans for dinner. Though he was more selective at the buffet than usual and didn't eat as much as before, he participated in the conviviality of the occasion with as much gusto as he could muster. Afterward, in the lobby he invited me to manipulate a mechanical gadget that was reputed to measure one's libido. When it spit out a high level for me, he said, "Now I know where I got mine."

Those who knew David found his humor to be a delight. On one of my March 19th birthdays, a birth date which his son, Frank, shares with me, David sent me a birthday card with a depiction on the front of it of Dopey with his mammoth ears. In the card Dopey is saying, "Pop, I'd have to be Dopey to forget to wish you your happiest birthday yet! Happy birthday!" Beneath the words David wrote, "I just had to get this card, because Bernadette recently told me that Dopey reminded her of me. She said it was mainly the ears, so you should be able to identify with him also. I tried to call you last night (Tuesday) around 10:00 but got no answer. Little Frankie was going to wish you happy birthday and thank you for the thought, so I am saying it for him. I want to thank you, too, for sending him the card and for being such a beautiful father. Happy Birthday. Love, David" What wonderful words of love and life these were!

The day after our dinner out it was evident that David's energy had waned because of his cancer ordeal. Even so, he engaged in a lively conversation with Linda. They shared experiences they had together some of which Jean and I had not heard about before. Before he excused himself for a nap, I showed him the Dopey card and a high school picture which together with a listing of his many accomplishments and involvements had appeared in the paper when we moved to a new parish in Stevensville, MI. Among the accomplishments listed was the award given him in his sophomore year for being Bronson High School's "Best Actor". His acting ability was put to good use as an adult living in London, KY. This for him became a special ministry. Though he would not have used the words "special ministry", in reality it was because of the lives of many children and their parents which he touched in positive ways.

One family event which we recalled before leaving to return home was our trip years before to Mackinac Island, an island in Michigan on the Lake Huron side of the Straits of Mackinac. While we were enjoying a carriage ride with other tourists, David spoke up and said, "We had to take all our money out of the bank so we could go on this trip." Indeed it was a major event in many wonderful ways for the Phillips family. I believe that our discussion of that very happy occasion triggered a decision by David and his family which later on I'll describe as a key happening in his faith search.

On May 13th, the three of us left to return to Michigan. The next day, I was scheduled for a heart catherization. But before we left, I proudly gave to David a copy of my book on Revelation, Fire From The Sky. He was pleased to receive the book he had often asked about, even though he and I knew that it was highly unlikely that he would be able to concentrate enough to read the whole book. Bernadette said that perhaps they could read parts of the book together.

Other wonderful words which celebrated their continuing love and life were written to Bernadette on the occasion of Memorial Day. The words themselves say so much, and need no comment.

"1997

Even though it is Memorial Day, I think it is appropriate

to celebrate that which is alive and flourishing. The love we share will never die, for it is far too powerful and all encompassing. Few will ever experience this depth and that is very unfortunate, for there is no greater force.

I never would have shared this without you and for that I am eternally grateful. So when this time rolls around next May, give me a little pause, a little kiss and a little smile. I will be there with you.

All my heart, David XXX"

On May 27th prior to the Memorial Day referred to in David's loving words to Bernadette, Jean and I left for David's London, KY, home. He was a lover of many styles of music, so we took with us a CD a friend of his thought might bring David a message of hope. It contains a concert called "Our God Is With Us", featuring the Azusa Pacific University Choir and Orchestra. The faith-filled music focused on the truth of God's incarnational presence in Jesus. At one point in the concert a soloist sings concerning God, "He appeared in a cloud of light, but no one had seen His face." Then the concert soloist sings concerning the revelation of God that later was visible in the person of Jesus. This was a fulfillment of the prophecy in Isaiah 7:14: "The Lord, himself, will give you a sign: The virgin will be with child and will give birth to a son, and will call him

41

Immanuel." Immanuel means "God with us". Jesus came to earth as God in the flesh in order that through faith in Him we might be reconciled to God and thus be at peace with God. This was the living truth that we prayed David would embrace so that Jesus' spirit might live within him, giving him complete confidence in God's love that comes from the full assurance of personal salvation. Having this assurance results in a great peace that can transform one from being a victim to being a victor. Would our time to be spent with David contribute to that transformation?

Our stay with David was only for two days. But I believe those two days would be the key to the transformation for which we prayed. On June 1st, we were due to attend our grandson's high school graduation celebration scheduled to be held at Haymount United Methodist Church in Fayetteville, NC. Andrew's graduation was scheduled for the following Wednesday. Though the preceding time with David covered a short span of time, I know in retrospect that what occurred then was basic to his later commitment of faith that brought him peace.

On our last day with David, May 29th, I drove him to Corbin, KY, where he received a radium treatment. Also, I went with him and one of his friends who helped him finalize a business transaction related to his sign business. This transaction marked a closure for David, the sign-maker. But what occurred the previous evening marked the beginning for David the seeker after truth. On the evening of May 28th, David exhibited sharpness of wit as he genuinely enjoyed taking Jean and myself to a German restaurant that had opened a short time before in the London area. He saw this addition as a real asset to the community. He bantered with the restaurant employees and discussed the German menu with us.

Our visit at the restaurant provided us with a prime opportunity to talk about the Christian faith, particularly the atonement for sin which Jesus made possible by His death on the cross. We discussed the necessity and importance of Jesus' sacrifice of Himself on the cross, in relationship to both the holiness and love of God. I explained in the words of Psalm 85:10 that "righteousness and peace kiss each other" at the cross where Jesus laid down His life as a sacrifice for our sins. "God is holy", I said. "Therefore, we who are sinful can not make atonement, or pay the price for our sins. But Jesus who was without sin offered himself as a perfect sacrifice for our sins. When we believe that Jesus died on the cross for us and accept His sacrifice for our sins, then we are justified, meaning that we are declared righteous based on the merits of Jesus. So we are at peace with God. Thus at the cross 'righteousness and peace kiss each other.'"

David listened carefully as Jean and I talked about God's love for him. We also told him that though we may not understand all the mysteries of faith, when we seek the Lord and call upon Him, He will hear us and make Himself known to us. So we urged him to continue his search for truth based on the promise of Matthew 7:7: "Ask and it will be given you; seek and you will find; knock and the door will be opened to you."

Before we left for North Carolina, David gave us the most wonderful note which he had written on May 28th following our dinner conversation:

"Dear Mom and Dad,

I want to thank you for the conversation we had over dinner this evening. Your wisdom and abundant love proved to be inspiring and

43

enlightening as it always has, even on those occasions when I may not have acknowledged it.

I doubt that I am any closer to understanding the over-all picture and purpose of why life unfolds as it does, but you have shown me that it is imperative to continue the search for that understanding. If I do continue the search for the truth, realizing that there are many things I may never understand, and acknowledge that fact; then the battle has nearly been won and I am on my way. Once I cease trying, I am doomed. Have no fear, I will not stop the search. The truth will come to light and it will all come together.

I love you both very much,

David"

These words of David were indeed wonderful words of love and life.

Chapter 9

Looking at Peace

"Have no fear, I will not stop the search. The truth will come to light and it will all come together." These last words in David's note were reassuring as we left for North Carolina. After Andrew's graduation, we left for home on June 8, 1997. On our way home, we stopped at Jean's sister's apartment in Sheffield Lake, Ohio. We were shocked to learn from Hazel's son that she was in a coma due to an aneurysm and was at the Cleveland Clinic Hospital from which she had retired several years before as an X-ray technician. Her prognosis was not good. After stopping to see her, we stayed in her apartment overnight; and after another visit the next day, left for our home in Niles, Michigan.

After I arrived home, I decided to write David a letter concerning my conversion at age six at a Vacation Bible School. My concern was that despite his keen mind, perhaps our conversation at the restaurant was too theological. So I wrote the simple story of my response to visible images of the human heart. The first heart shown by the teacher was a black heart representing sin. Then Miss Kenyon, the teacher, talked about sins children commit such as lying, stealing, swearing, etc.. Then she placed a red heart over the black one, representing the blood of Jesus that He shed upon the cross because of our sins. Finally, she placed a white heart over the red one, representing the pure hearts we are given when we tell the Lord we are sorry for our sins. When she asked us to come forward and kneel at the altar rail if we wanted to have a pure heart, I went forward with the others. When we knelt, I wept because I knew that as a six year old I had lied, stolen and often had sworn. Then Miss Kenyon led us in a prayer in which we asked Jesus who died on the cross because of our sins to come and live in our lives, so that through His shed blood, our black hearts might be white. I truly believed that Jesus had washed away my sins and felt a great joy and peace. My parents who were not Christians were amazed by my changed behavior.

After I mailed the letter, I prayed that God would use the simple visual message to help David, the artist and sign maker, experience the peace and assurance that would come from believing that Jesus died for him that he might be forgiven and have eternal life.

On June 11, Jean and I went to the West Michigan Annual Conference of the United Methodist Church held at Albion College in Albion, MI. There we sold signed copies of my book, Fire From The Sky. We had not been there long before we received word that Hazel had died. We left immediately for Sheffield Lake, OH. When we looked out her window overlooking Lake Erie the next day, we saw a single sea gull. Was the lone bird there to mourn as well? In our hearts we wondered if it came to represent the many gulls she loved who were often seen in the vicinity of her apartment.

As a part of our preparation for the day of celebration when through tears we celebrated the glorious home going of Hazel, Jean wrote a beautiful eulogy that was read by the pastor of Hazel's church at the service held on Saturday, June 14, 1997. Her prayers, her calls, her cards, her acts of service, and most of all her life were and are an inspiration to all who knew her.

When we returned home after Hazel's Memorial Service, a Father's Day card awaited me in our mail-box. This card for Father's Day, June 15, 1997, was the last written special greeting from David. On its cover was an empty chair on a porch overlooking a body of water on which sail boats were depicted. Next to the chair was a table on which there was a closed book, binoculars, and what looked like an untouched glass of lemonade. Likely this card was not chosen to represent an impending absence, but the date of Father's Day in 1997 was exactly one month before the death of my son.

David wrote inside the card:

"Dear Dad,

So much has happened in the past couple of months that I am at a total loss for words.

All I can do is to express my undying love and gratitude once again, along with the knowledge there is a greater purpose somewhere in this seeming madness.

I suppose this will have to do for now. Tomorrow is another day.

Thank you and God bless.

Love and Kisses,

David

Happy Father's Day!!"

Indeed, what David said in the card helped make it a happy Father's Day. Never before had he spoken of a "greater purpose". Nor had he ever said, "God Bless". Despite the "seeming madness" of his condition, no doubt referring to the ravages of his body and the rapid depletion of his ability to work and enjoy relationships to the full in various pursuits, he seemed to sense the presence of a God who has a benign purpose. The reference to a Divine Being who enters into the experiences of people would not have been made two months prior to the sending of the Father's Day card. In the weeks to come David would experientially, in part at least, become aware of the "greater purpose" at work in his life. This would be a prelude to the time when in heavenly places he would "know fully" even as God fully knew about his spiritual birth pains during the time of his terminal illness, I Corinthians 13:12.

Reynolds Price in a letter he wrote to a young man stricken with cancer said on page 66 of his book Letter To A Man In The Fire that it was his hope that the young man in "some form of conscious and immortal life" would "comprehend and accomplish what may be dark and closed to you here and now." This is the hope of every believer, a hope given by God's Word and confirmed by the Holy Spirit.

The popular movie star, Brad Pitt, said that he was hearing the ticking of a personal clock as he was approaching his 35th birthday. In the November 22, 1998, copy of the "South Bend Tribune" he is cited as saying in what he called "a great line" in the boxing film he was making with Edward Norton: "This is your life and it's ending one day at a time." The truth of these words was even more poignant for my son who because of his terminal cancer sought after God who revealed to him a "greater purpose" at work in his life.

This sense of a greater purpose was a God-given gift that David received. To what end then was cancer for David a contributing factor to God's greater purpose for his life? We must begin answering that question by asking another one, namely: What does God intend that a greater purpose accomplish when it is associated with suffering? The intention is that the greater purpose which rides on the back of the discipline of suffering will be realized through divine grace which makes possible peace with God. This truth is the thrust of what the writer of "Hebrews" says: "God disciplines us for our own good, that we may share in His holiness. No discipline seems pleasant at the time, but painful. Later on, however, it produces a harvest of righteousness and peace..." Hebrews 12:10b-11. One endowed with God's holiness and peace is no longer afraid of what the future holds.

Is it not paradoxical that evil suffered, in David's case cancer, is often the condition of one who experiences God's gift of peace? His description of his physical condition as "this seeming madness" is so appropriate because God could have made a world where there is neither moral evil, or evil suffered. But in David's words we see the problem of evil present with us. We do not find in David's words bitterness, nor did I ever hear him question God or charge Him as being an agent of evil. If it is true that he never questioned God, this is a miracle of God's grace. For him out of evil suffered came good.

Brian Davies, Professor of Philosophy at Fordham University in New York City, in the book he edited entitled, <u>Philosophy A Guide to the</u>

Subject of Religion said he sees the problem of evil as an invitation "to reflect on the mystery of divinity, something which serves to remind us that God is nothing less than the beginning and the end of all things, the source from which everything we can understand derives its existence." This reflection on "the mystery of divinity" of which Davies speaks is certain to raise questions concerning God's justice even though evil is often the result of man's actions or inactions. On the basis of God's revealed Word, I believe His justice is in accordance with His declared will related to His covenant purposes, including His work of salvation in Jesus Christ. Impartial retribution, or some humanly determined ideal of fairness is not the basis of God's dealings with his children. Rather, He gives to His creatures in accordance with their spiritual needs related to their possible place in the covenant community of faith.

What is our greatest need? A funeral director who at the time was living in the sunset of his life once asked me that question. Before I could answer, he told me that he believed it is peace. Knowing that the New Testament speaks of two kinds of peace, namely, "peace with God" and "the peace of God", I told him that I agreed with him. In Colossians 1:20 we read that peace with God has been made possible through the shedding of the blood of God's Son on the cross. The word translated "peace" comes from the Greek verb meaning to build together that which has been separated. Sin separated the human race from God who is holy. But when by faith we accept the self-sacrifice of Jesus upon the cross for our sins, then we are justified, that is declared righteous. So, therefore, "we have peace with God through our Lord Jesus Christ." Romans 5:1. After we are reconciled to God, and hence are at peace with Him, there will be times when anxiety will deprive us of the "peace of God". In Philippians 4:6,7 we learn that through prayer "the peace of God, which transcends all understanding, will guard your hearts and your minds in Christ Jesus." So even after we have been reconciled to God, there will be times when through spiritual discipline we will need to cultivate the "peace of God".

My first concern for David was that he have "peace with God". Now I am privileged to tell the story of how David affirmed that he, indeed, was at "peace with God". Prior to David's affirmation of peace, you may recall that I told a colleague of mine in the ministry of the church that I had "peace, great peace" that all would be well with David. Without ceasing, I prayed that he, indeed, would make his "peace with God."

As mentioned before, it was in our conversation the day after Mother's Day that we recalled the great time which our family had on Mackinac Island when David was a young boy. Likely it was this conversation that quickened in him a desire to revisit that part of Michigan. On the way to that destination, Bernadette and David went to a drug rehabilitation center in Fort Wayne, IN, to visit their son, Frank, who had chosen to receive help for recovery at the center. This visit to see Frank marked the occasion of an open house at which they enjoyed a barbecue and had the opportunity to meet the man in charge, as well as other personnel who worked at the center. Following this experience, Frank was granted permission to accompany his parents to our home in Michigan. The three of them arrived on June 22nd. Jean and I offered our downstairs bedroom to Bernadette and David, but he insisted on climbing the stairs to the familiar room where he had stayed before when he had visited us. David appeared to be quite energetic. His smiles and laughter reminded me of far lighter occasions when everything seemed right with the world and ourselves. Though at times it seemed like another happy Michigan reunion, the reality of life under fire could not escape us.

The next day was a beautiful warm day. In the afternoon David enjoyed relaxing on a lounge outdoors. On my way back from the mailbox at the end of the driveway, I said to him as he lounged in the sun, "Boy, that's the life." We both laughed, but I wished those words had never been spoken for my heart was broken by the thought of his terminal illness.

I felt my flippant words were ill chosen when the thought crossed my mind that this was likely, and indeed was, David's last visit to our home. Regardless of how long his future in this world would be, his love for us would never die. A reminder of his love resides in a beautiful gift for Jean and myself which occupies the central place on our fireplace mantel. The gracious gift which David had mailed to us is a continuous reminder that love for one another is the essence of what the life that is worth living is all about. This reminder is a white Haeger designed sculpture, copyrighted 1996, composed of a man and woman sitting facing one another with knees bent, arms and feet entwined, and heads bowed. This sculpture depicting reverent love is also a reinforcement of Jean's belief and mine that David's terminal cancer was a blessing because it opened the way for his experience of God's redeeming love. We know that his life from the time of his baptism to his death at the age of 43 was a saga of God's faithful love. Because David lived a life of love and died a child of God born of water and the Spirit, John 3:5, many have been blessed. Among those blessed are his parents, sister and brother.

After their time of lounging, David and Frank came into the living room where I had been looking at the mail. The artistic reminder of the centrality of love which I just described was in the place it occupies to this day. Our conversation was more serious now, but still not without lighter moments. A question I directed to David dealt with how he would like to be remembered. After a time of sharing thoughts, I said, "David has lived a life of dignity and now he is dying with dignity." There was no verbal response from anyone in the room, but David looked at me with eyes reflecting the love that was so much a part of his inner being. It was a peaceful moment; but an emotional moment, too, as Frank sought to quietly conceal his feelings by slowly walking out of the room.

Later that evening of June 23rd, David and Bernadette were on their way for a time together at Mackinaw City where they looked forward to some good days together in an idyllic setting. Frank left for Fort Wayne.

Despite some flare up heart episodes during David's illness, my heart's condition at this time was of little concern to me. But on June 26th, I had an appointment to see my cardiologist for tests. As a result of findings, I was scheduled for surgery on July 28th.

After David and Bernadette got settled in a cabin which was right on Lake Michigan and in the environs of Mackinaw City, they had four great days enjoying the sun and water. Then we received a call from Bernadette saying that David's condition had quickly deteriorated. Following a book signing in Bronson, MI on Saturday, June 28th, we left for Mackinaw City. We stayed overnight in a motel located in Big Rapids not far from Ferris State University from which Linda had graduated. Based on

Bernardette's directions, the next day we had no difficulty finding the cabin.

When we entered the door of the cabin on Sunday, June 29th, Bernadette told us David was resting. I walked quietly over to his bed and immediately David wakened, sat up, and with a beautiful glow on his face greeted me with the words, "Peace, great peace!" I said, "David, then you are trusting in the Lord?" He replied, "Yes, I am." I knew that all our prayers related to David's spiritual condition based on his commitment to the Lord had been answered. Immediately, I recalled what I had said to my ministerial friend regarding David's spiritual welfare. I had told him, "I have peace, great peace, that all will be well with David." I had never ever used the words, "Peace, great peace" in a conversation with David. Yet he affirmed his faith in the Lord by using those very words I had previously used in my conversation with a friend. God's mercy, faithfulness and love are boundless! After David's personal search for truth prompted and directed by the Holy Spirit in answer to the prayers of many of God's people, he had been reconciled to God and now had experienced "peace with God" - the peace that the Apostle Paul wrote about in Romans 5:1. I felt an affinity with the Apostle who in writing to the Galatians in Galatians 4:19 spoke of his "pains of childbirth until Christ is formed in you." My heart truly leaped for joy.

Jean and I stayed overnight in another cabin close to David's. The next day he indicated that he was ready to return to his home in London, KY. David's son Paul and his wife Lisa had driven from their home in Kentucky to Mackinaw City to be with David and Bernadette. David was placed in their vehicle in a prone position so that his ride home would be as comfortable as possible. He never did go by boat to Mackinac Island. His experience as a youngster on the island was still a fond memory, but the good time he and his wife had together before other family members joined them was much more than just a pleasant memory.

Later we learned that the four of them drove through to Kentucky, stopping at Georgetown, KY for what I believe was David's last meal of solid food which included a hamburger. After his trip to Michigan and his glorious affirmation of peace, David returned home to die. But his death would be a gateway to the realm of eternal day. Jean and I returned to Michigan. We, too, were at peace knowing that David's impending death no longer had power over him.

When David arrived home from Mackinaw City, he had a surprise awaiting him. Linda and John found a way to enter David's locked home. The reunion was a happy one even though John and Linda experienced shock when they saw the toll taken on his body as a result of his cancer. The once handsome, quick-witted young man was not the brother they were accustomed to seeing. Though not totally bereft of his sense of humor, his green eyes did not emit their usual sparkle. He went through the motions of normalcy; but even when he shared part of his attention with grandson, Brandon, as he played with his toys, his zest was not nearly as pronounced as before.

David had looked back on days when summer was kinder, at a place where he found he still had enough energy to engage in muted play. That place was Mackinaw City. But before leaving a place of yesteryear's fun, he also looked at the shadow of death. Then he left for home to touch the ground where he had known a stable life. That ground he knew would soon be the place where his body would be reduced to ashes through cremation. This he had accepted knowing he was at peace.

On the second and last day of the reunion, David by words and mannerisms gave Linda and John signs that he was nonplused to the point of anger that his body was still saying, "You've got to hang around longer." So while the reunion was characterized by intense love and joy, it was tinctured by a sadness that he and his sister and brother could not have imagined would occur. The "what ifs" and the "if onlys" had already begun to cross the minds of John and Linda. But despite that, in the days to come Easter's "Alleluia, Jesus is risen" would give them the assurance of a glorious reunion yet to be based on Jesus' promise, "Because I live, you also will live", John 14:19b.

On the evening of July 2nd, a call came informing us it had been determined that perhaps David had only two days to live. We left for Kentucky the 3rd. When Jean and I arrived on the morning of July 4th at David's beautiful setting overlooking a tranquil body of water nestled in a natural cavity with precipitous banks covered with a variety of trees on both sides, his home was enveloped in warm sunlight. To our surprise David was outdoors on the patio with other members of his family including Brandon in whom he took great delight. The sting of death seemed far removed from the idyllic scene. The pool table, which David had wanted for some time, occupied a chunk of space on the patio. For a brief time he got to enjoy the pastime it invited. During those difficult days which followed when he was in his bedroom barely existing with the dreaded cancer that gnawed at his mind and body, Frank and Paul relieved their stress by testing their skills as they aimed balls across the cushioned, green surface into accepting deep pockets.

When David greeted us with his customary warm smile, the thought did not occur to me that this might be the last time he would greet us outdoors on his patio. Even so, his disease was apparent. When I asked him if he knew it was the 4th of July, he responded, "So they told me." I asked him if he remembered when our family on the 4th of July many years ago visited Jefferson's home in Montecello. He nodded. His words were few. Our conversation, short-lived. He then retired to his bedroom. We had seen his winning smile and felt the warmth of his love. But this would be his last venture in the out-of-doors that he loved so much. We were now jolted into the realization that his days were numbered.

The "peace of God" from this time to the end of David's earthly sojourn at times seemed remote. The expectation of possibly two more days of life actually stretched to two more weeks. Though David had made his "peace with God", the restless nights when he would often babble incoherently were nightmares. Even so, there were moments during the day that were more precious than gold. Before I describe a prime moment which for me, paradoxically, was both wrenching and relieving, I wish to emphasize that David was both lucid and free of pain. His mind was not focusing on exit as much as entrance. The moment of which I now write occurred two days before his spirit flew into a new and glorious realm of reality. His words indicated that he was ready to experience what the writer of Hebrews in chapter 4, verse 9, refers to as a peace that "remains".

As we were alone in his bedroom, David asked, "When do I go back to start?" I sensed that the question was couched in the language of board games that he had played as a boy. My heart leaped with joy even in this somber moment as I sensed David's use of the word "start" indicated he viewed death as the beginning of a desired venture. My response to his question was, "David, I don't think it will be long. Let us pray that will be the case; so you may enter into the Realm Of Eternal Light." Then I said, "Please pray with me." The exact words of my (our) prayer are not important; for the prayer was composed, in the words of St. Paul, "of groanings that cannot be uttered." But the interpretation that comes to me now goes like this: "Lord, you have given David a good life, but now he is ready to enter into the fullness of Your presence. Lord, may it not be long before he enters into the Realm Of Eternal Light. Amen." He then rested peacefully. Two days later on July 15 at 6:35 p.m., he entered the Realm Of Eternal Light where God's glory is supreme and where David would forever be at peace.

Chapter 10

Looking At Providence

A truth that we'll never fully be able to comprehend in this life is that God is actively at work in nature and history not only in a general sense, but in our personal lives as well. Furthermore, there is a divine purpose involved in those workings, even when related to our experience of evil and suffering. This purpose is never definable as cut and dried determinism, because we still have a freedom of choice. These are some of the particulars usually identified with the Christian doctrine of providence.

David in his search for truth had become aware of the mystery of a divine purpose at work despite the limits of human understanding. In his Father's Day card he had spoken of the "seeming madness" he had experienced through his incapacitating suffering over the previous "couple months". Later on in the note I previously cited which he wrote to his mother and myself he said,… "there are many things that I may never understand, and acknowledge that fact..." Yet, despite this, he wrote concerning his "knowledge" that "there is a greater purpose". Finally, he made a choice to "trust in the Lord" as he declared at Mackinaw City. He experienced "peace, great peace" through his acceptance of Jesus as the One through whom God's purpose is experienced.

I believe the reader of my account of David's final days would do well to consider how in his story, and potentially in the story of every human being, one through spiritual eyes may discern the outworking of God's providence. While I invite the reader to see through the lens of my theology, others may discern much of the same truth which I declare through the lens of different understandings. At any rate, if you wish to further pursue the topic of providence, you may wish to consult a reputable reference work. For a succinct, and for me a satisfying description of the Christian doctrine of providence, I highly recommend Geoffrey W. Bromiley's contribution under the heading of "Providence" found in The International Standard Bible Encyclopedia, Volume 3, copyrighted in 1986 by William B. Eerdmans Publishing Company. On page 1024 in that volume the General Editor, G. W. Bromiley, wrote concerning providence: "The doctrine of providence maintains that there is a purpose behind not merely the existence but also the course of the world. The world is not just a chance event. Its story both in nature and history is no meaningless muddle on which at best a meaning has to be imposed. Its happenings and developments do not simply occur, following no plan and leading to no goal. The world was from the very first planned for a purpose; and although the fall and sin of man have introduced a disruptive element, what takes place still serves this overruling purpose."

Later on the same page, Bromiley states: "The overruling purpose of God in Christ is man in fellowship with God and with fellow men. The supreme story of the world is the attainment of the purpose in spite of its original frustration. The task of providence is the shaping of natural and historical events in such a way that the purpose is fulfilled. Its fulfillment is in and by the special work of God, which reaches its culmination in the vicarious life and death and resurrection of Jesus Christ, in the application of this work in individual lives, and in the final establishment of His Kingdom at the Parousia."

The last quotation from Bromiley speaks of the "special work of God, which reaches its culmination in the vicarious life and death and resurrection of Jesus Christ, in the application of this work in individual lives..." That application for David resulted in his "peace with God." But would this same Jesus Christ in whom he found peace also be sufficient for him during the last very trying days of his life? Would God in His sovereign providence translate the "peace with God" which was now his as a result of his faith in Jesus, into the "peace of God' which would sustain him during the final period of his life when all the demons of hell would be arrayed against him in his helpless physical state? Would the word of comfort that Jesus gave his disciples when they were confused and barely able to face their future find its application in David's life during those pitiful times of his weakness? The word of Jesus of which I speak is found in John 14:27: "Peace I leave with you; my peace I give you. I do not give to you as the world gives. Do not let your hearts be troubled and do not be afraid." Would the reality of Christ as David's peace as stated by Paul in Ephesians 2:13-14a be his experience during his last days? Paul wrote, "But now in Christ Jesus you who once were far away have been brought near through the blood of Christ. For he himself is our peace." Paul in writing to the Philippians in the epistle by the same name in chapter 1, verse 6, spoke of a confidence that the Lord's followers may have in the words, "...he who began a good work in you will carry it on to completion until the day of Christ Jesus." By "the day of Christ Jesus" he means the time of His return to earth (Parousia) which will mark the end of history as we know it.

The process of God's saving initiative began on the path of the miraculous. The incarnation, God taking the form of human flesh in Jesus Christ, and the resurrection of Jesus in a historical time frame are absolutely miraculous in that natural causes could not produce such results. Likewise, a personal transcendent God is the sole cause of new birth in the life of the believer. The same Divine Being is the sole source of the revelation of the mystery of God in the person of Jesus as indicated by the word of Jesus to Peter when he bore witness to the Divine Messiahship of Jesus. At that time Jesus said to Peter, "Blessed are you, Simon son of Jonah, for this was not revealed to you by man, but by my Father in heaven." Matthew 16:17. These miraculous revelations of the Gospel form the core of the Lord's continuing presence in the lives of believers.

When one is on the cutting edge of divine intention, the possibilities of life are limitless. The prayers of caring believers are often the catalyst for the phenomenon of God's personal, providential ordering of events at propitious times in the lives of believers utilizing natural, and at times supernatural means. As with Peter, through prayer earth's shackles fall away. Acts 12:5-7.

Does this make God a divine bellhop who does just what we want Him to do for us? No, just the opposite is the case. God takes the initiative to reveal His awesomeness and the path by which we bring glory to His holy will and name. Sometimes the path is one of suffering that through accompanying prayer ushers one into the loving presence of the Majesty on High.

The Danish philosopher and theologian, Sören Kierkegaard (1813-1855), emphasized that there can be no true religious existence without the free choice of self-commitment to God. Not even alternatives such as commitment to beauty and moral respect will suffice. Because man needs God, he needs to take the leap of faith recognizing that God alone is God. David had taken that leap of faith as evidenced by what he said at Mackinaw City. As a result, he had "peace with God". He was reconciled with God, because he was justified by faith. Furthermore, he had received the "peace of God", because of the presence of the Holy Spirit in his life giving him hope even in the midst of whatever trial he would endure before being called to his heavenly home.

What role would the "peace of God" play in David's life the last two weeks after he returned from Mackinaw City? A truly amazing statement is made in Colossians 3:15 where we learn that the "peace of God" can "rule" in one's heart. The Greek word translated rule is a term borrowed from the athletic arena where contests occurred in which an arbiter, or umpire, often was needed to make decisions related to athletic events. During the latter period of David's life, raging feelings and inner clashings of emotions and thoughts were taking place in his heart and mind robbing him of sleep; and so it appeared, any resemblance of even peace itself. Could it be that "the peace of God" under those circumstances was no longer operative? When love and fear, faith and distrust, awareness and concern were part of a chaotic mix was there no peace present to give him inner harmony? In times of anguish and chaos, what feelings really reigned? Where was peace that Paul said could act as an umpire to settle clashes and as an arbiter destroy skepticism? Could peace at such a time establish feelings of well being so essential to a sense of hope? What about those who heard and saw what was transpiring, must they just observe with a plastic indifference because of their inability to change anything, or could they demonstrate concerned love and soothe the painful passions? Oh Christ, where is your peace? God, do I faintly hear the mystifying words from the cross which no human being can fully understand, "My God, my God, why have you forsaken me?" Matthew 27:46.

Some answers, partial at best, but driven by honest intent, and containing truth that one day will fully blossom, I'll attempt to give. But even in an attempt to answer questions of an ultimate nature, I cringe as Job must have when God asked him, "Do you know the laws of the heavens? Can you set up God's dominion over the earth?" Job 38:33. So when I answered the telephone call from Bernadette the evening of July 2nd, and heard her say that a Hospice worker said, based on David's condition, he might have as few as two more days to live, I felt numb with shock. The next day Jean and I left after informing John and Linda and gathering things we thought were needed for an indefinite stay. One item we took which we did not take previously was a booklet that seeks to explain death to children entitled "Water Bugs and Dragonflies". We thought it might be helpful for Brandon to hear the booklet read. On the way we discussed the beauty and value of the booklet's message for adults like ourselves as well.

God in His wisdom gave David two more weeks, rather than two days. For David there were times when two weeks seemed like an eternity. There is a benediction in Paul's epistle to the Romans, chapter 15 and verse 13 that he and the members of his family needed during the days of his final ordeal. It goes like this: "May the God of hope fill you with all joy and peace as you trust in him, so that you may overflow with hope by the power of the Holy Spirit."

Where was the joy of which Paul spoke? He used the word 21 times in his epistles, including situations in which joy seemed to be a remote possibility. Where was the joy during the night hours when David's mind raced with thoughts pertaining to his work? He rambled aloud about jobs to be done, materials to be ordered, contracts to be signed, etc.. Jean and I sought to assure him that everything was okay. Provision would be made for his concerns. We took turns with Bernadette spending the night in his bedroom where sleep was a rare commodity for him and us.

One day when Jean and I were with him in his bedroom simply enjoying being near him and trying to be cheerful, he asked the question, "Where is the joy?" We didn't try to answer his question with a logical statement, because it was impossible to do so. We took in response to his question this as an opportunity to reassure him with hugs, kisses and words of endearment that spoke of how deeply we loved him. The "peace of God" through what the Apostle Paul referred to as the "love, which binds everything together in perfect harmony" reigned in those precious moments. Colossians 3:14.

On one of the first days of the last two weeks we found David on the floor by his bed in a near-lotus position. He had tried to make his way to the bathroom but got no further. We told him that he looked like Ghandi. In his weakened condition he managed to laugh, as he did at other times on several occasions when laughter hardly seemed to be the order of the day. Again, the "peace of God" prevailed.

One personal feeling that I wrestled with during this period of time was guilt. A couple of times I took a break and walked and walked in the beautiful Kentucky countryside. Questions at the time I asked myself were of this order: As a pastor was I so concerned about the needs of my congregation that I failed to take note of David's needs related to how much he needed my presence and concern? Did I make known to him how much I truly loved him? If I had been more understanding and solicitous of his spiritual needs would he have been spared the addiction that had contributed to his physical and spiritual malaise? One day during the time when one of the Hospice workers was attending to his physical needs, I heard coming from David words that for me were healing words. The worker spoke to him about how wonderful it was that I was there for him giving physical and spiritual support. She said how great it was that he could count on my love. David's reply was, "He's really helped me." The "peace of God' that was sustaining David also gave me strength and a sense of gratitude that his length of days extended beyond the number expected, so that both of us in a time of agony experienced a bond of love that otherwise would not have been known with such great intensity.

Jean and I both have often mentioned how blessed we were to be with David during the most trying period of his life. Jean's loving, daily physical and spiritual care for him conjures up for me unforgettable scenes of her compassionate concern, strength, patience and skills. David's siblings, Linda and John, even during the process of their grieving were pillars of strength for David, Jean and myself. A scene Jean and I will always remember was one that encapsuled the love between Bernadette and David. It occurred a few days before he died. She rubbed his forehead and spoke soothing and loving words interspersed several times with the description, "David, my knight in shining armor." He was basking in a kind of paradise they had experienced together in many wonderful ways during their marriage. Paul and Frank were also there for him. Frank pitched in by caring for the household grounds through his physical labors, and Paul was Johnny on the spot acting as a host when people called, or doing with alacrity and skill whatever the moment demanded. Added to the supportive family was Bernadette's saintly mother, Beatrice, who was queen of the kitchen and a tower of spiritual strength. Bernadette's siblings, some of whom were able to spend short periods in London, and others who kept in contact by phone also were a source of encouragement. Lisa, Paul's wife, in her wise and quiet way made life better by her presence in the house high on the hill in Fisherman's Cove. Many extended members of the family gave assistance and food, as well as whatever else was needed. With all of this loving support dark days were made brighter for the "peace of God" came to life through their love.

I have saved for last a description of a scene which for me was a prime manifestation of the "peace of God." David glowed with a vivacity which I can only describe as a miracle of transfiguration. It took place three days before he died. Brandon was given the opportunity to enter David's bedroom to spend some time alone with him. To my amazement, David who for days had been in a prone position, sat up in bed with Brandon beside him. David was very weak, because for days he had been taking virtually no nourishment in any form. Yet they were sitting up together, talking, and laughing, and smiling at one another. I caught a glimpse of them from some distance. I have no idea what they talked about, and in a way am glad I didn't, because this was their sacred moment of transfiguration. But this I saw: The "peace of God" which is the supreme manifestation of God's providential presence was there. David's face was aglow, and Brandon who at his age scarcely understood what was happening was at ease in the presence of the grandfather he loved. What greater expression of the "peace of God" in human experience could there be than this. Providence was a reality to the eyes of faith at a time when strictly from a human perspective hope seemed absent because of the frowning chill of impending death.

Chapter 11

Looking for Holy Signs

After my lofty pronouncements about providence and the "peace of God", the reader may think I was whistling in the dark, because I'm about to confess that such concepts were usually far from my mind during David's final difficult days. Only in retrospect do I clearly see the hand of God at work. Does this not tell us something about our enmeshment in time which often blinds us to the reality of eternity? And so we fall into the pattern of Plato's cave where it seemed that the shadows on the walls were the only reality.

In Matthew's Gospel, chapter 16 in the first four verses, we are told that the Pharisees and Sadducees tested Jesus "by asking him to show them a sign from heaven." Jesus replied, "When evening comes, you say, 'It will be fair weather, for the sky is red,' and in the morning, 'Today it will be stormy, for the sky is red and overcast.' You know how to interpret the appearance of the sky, but you cannot interpret the signs of the times. A wicked and adulterous generation looks for a miraculous sign, but none will be given it except the sign of Jonah." The sign of Jonah indicated that life prevailed when Jonah emerged alive from the mouth of the great fish, even though only the possibility of death seemed evident after he was swallowed by the fish. Death seemed ready to swallow David; so we engaged in a death vigil, forgetting that in reality it was a life vigil, because of the resurrection of Jesus. So in this segment of Cancer's Seeming Madness I shall call attention to Holy Signs, which like the

69

natural signs in the heavens to which Jesus alluded, were present for those who had eyes to see them. I am now referring to the period of July 4-15, 1997, prior to David's death, and during the days prior to his Memorial Service. Much of that time through July 13th in the daytime, David generally was calm and appreciative of the presence of family members and persons from Hospice who ministered so tenderly and skillfully to his physical and emotional needs. For a young man who had been so self-reliant his gratitude evident in his total dependency upon the ministrations of others was a Holy Sign.

As before mentioned, this general calmness did not persist during the nighttime hours. Short periods of quiet were interrupted by noisy bursts of random words related mostly to disconnected work concerns that turned over in David's mind. Almost as persistent as his outbursts, were the strangely raucous though somewhat melodic croaking of frogs on the nearby water-front who seemed to be engaging in a responsive ritual. It is no wonder that when we saw one another's bleary eyes the next morning, that the words, "Good morning" sometimes stuck in our throats. The goodness of each day centered in helping the young man we loved, and even sharing with him at times some smiles and light moments along with the pain we all felt. Knowing David was grateful that we were a part of a team of care-givers not only made life more bearable for him and us, but even worthwhile. This too was a Holy Sign greatly enhanced by Jesus, our great High Priest, to whom we often turned knowing that he was "touched with the feeling of our infirmities." Hebrews 4:15.

David took great pride in Brandon. Whenever David is seen in a photograph with Brandon, his face beams. One year he brought him to the

Scott family reunion, Scott being Jean's maiden name. It was evident in that setting that a warm friendship had also developed between Brandon and John. Brandon's love proved to be a touchstone of a special familial love. This familial love that endured in the face of the specter of death, and yes, beyond, was also a Holy Sign.

On Sunday, July 13, I attended Mass with Beatrice at St. William's Roman Catholic Church. The epistle reading that morning was from Ephesians 1:1-10. As I thought of David, verses 7-10 seemed especially applicable to his experience. They read: "In him (Jesus Christ) we have redemption through his blood, the forgiveness of sins, in accordance with the riches of God's grace that he lavished on us with all wisdom and understanding. And he made known to us the mystery of his will according to his good pleasure, which he purposed in Christ, to be put into effect when the times will have reached their fulfillment - to bring all things in heaven and on earth together under one head, even Christ." Is this not an expression of the "greater purpose" God had in mind for David of which he wrote in his Father's Day card to me? God's redemptive purpose realized in accordance with God's grace lavished on David "with all wisdom and understanding" which one day will "bring all things in heaven and on earth together under...Christ" had become the essence of the "greater purpose" given to David that resulted in his great peace and his being a part of God's family "under one head, even Christ." Father Stern's homily based on the Ephesian's passage was another Holy Sign.

Sunday, July 13, was also the day when as I previously indicated David asked, "When do I go back to start?" As the result of his question, I asked David to join with me in a prayer for his release from this life. His metaphor, of course, was related to board games. In a board game the directive to return to start is often a penalty. But sometimes with the directive there is a reward. In Monopoly when someone lands on "Chance" it may be announced that by returning to "Go" one collects $200. David, by his question, was saying that he was looking forward to a new beginning. While I am sure he wondered why his life which under the circumstances offered little that he could cherish had to continue in its state of great limitation and discomfort, I do not believe he was severely depressed. We also were grateful he did not suffer agonizing pain. But even so, he had every reason to desire release and entrance into a new life. In a state of painful love I joined my spirit with David's and offered a prayer for his release from this life which I truly believed was God's desire for him as well. The God-given ability to do this was a Holy Sign.

Marshall McLuhan, the Medium Is The Message Guru of the 1960's said that we need to "march backward into the future." In doing so, I believe we need to take a look at our roots, at the spiritual milieu that initially gave meaningful purpose to our lives. By doing this we may experience a renewed moral commitment that will rescue us from the sloughs of mediocrity and moral turpitude. At the very least it may prevent us from engaging in needless error and arrogant dalliance. But one must not dwell on the past, or consider it to be wholly sacrosanct. By marching backward into the future, we move in the direction of new discoveries, stimulating ideas, and worthwhile involvement in the ever unfolding drama of life.

David's Mackinaw experience was both a physical and spiritual experience of looking back that resulted in "peace with God", and peace within his inner being. His looking back while walking into the future reminded me of his deft high stepping as a drum major when he led the Bronson High School Band. During half-time at a football game, Jean and I were amazed by his ability to high step and make the turns as he walked backwards while leading the band. And the band marched with him. That's what made him a leader.

David's world after the Mackinaw trip was not the absurd, chaotic world Tom Wolf pictured at the end of his novel, A Man in Full. When David looked back, he reclaimed his covenant spiritual heritage given to him at the time of his baptism. All was right with his world. Peace prevailed. By expressing his desire to go back to start, David was saying that he was now ready in a new life to experience his new found peace in all its fullness. The expression of his acceptance of God's design for his future life was a Holy Sign.

After attending Mass on July 13 followed by my prayer with David that afternoon, Lisa suggested that I consider talking to David about something that may have been in that Sunday's edition of the "Lexington Herald Leader" that I thought might be of interest to him. She said that David often liked to talk about news developments and other articles that appeared in the Sunday paper. Though appreciative of Lisa's suggestion, I wondered whether that would be of interest to him when his physical condition would limit his attention span and his spirit was likely depleted. I saw functional impairment as a prohibitive factor no matter how appealing the idea might be. Nonetheless, later that day, I did pose the question. His response was "yes" he was interested, but that right then he didn't feel up to engaging in such a conversation. "Perhaps tomorrow," he said.

The next morning on July 14 after David's physical needs were cared for, he was ready to talk about whatever I thought might be of interest to him. I summarized for him an article written by David Sawyer the director of Berea College's service program. The article entitled "Pulling America Together" appeared under the Commentary section of the paper. The author saw a new spirit of personal and collective civic responsibility emerging in our country in the form of voluntary service directed toward solving perplexing problems in our nation. David who himself had volunteered service for the good of the community of which he was a part was pleased with what he heard.

But the other article we discussed really interested him. It was written by Ninie O'Hara a contributing columnist who was the publisher of "The Southeast Outlook" the weekly newspaper of Southeast Christian Church in Louisville. The article dealt with the CBS program, "Touched by an Angel." In the article she said that though Hollywood had been "touched" by the program, it still was clueless as to why it was so popular. She wrote, "What they (meaning critics of the program) don't understand is the Christian faith and what it means to believers. They don't understand it is real, not an 'escapist fantasy'. Christians know a personal God who loves and cares for them, and that knowledge is the single most important truth in their lives." I talked to David about how the program in Ninie's words, "..celebrates faith in a loving God who is involved in the lives of his children." As evidenced by David's listening and his own comments of affirmation of what was said in the article, the truth of God's love for him really resonated in his heart. This July 14th conversation was indeed another Holy Sign, a sign of what God had done and was about to do in David's life.

Our conversation on the morning of the 14th was the last conversational interchange I had with David, although the interchange of our spirits was still a reality. Later on that afternoon, David lapsed into what I would call a semi-coma. I have no way of judging whether he was still aware of our presence. Though his eyes were open, he seemed to be in a twilight zone which the Hospice worker saw as the beginning of his journey into another realm of life. His breathing at times was a little deep, but not because he was struggling to breathe. He was in no pain or distress. Nothing changed during the night that would indicate he would soon expire.

On his last day, Tuesday, July 15th, David's breathing was quieter, even and peaceful, as his spirit prepared to leave his body. In the afternoon when his breathing was even quieter, family members present gathered around his bed. There was Bernadette, Beatrice, Jean and myself. After a period of quietness, the Holy Spirit moved Jean and me to sing, "Peace, Peace, Wonderful Peace", and "Safe in the Arms of Jesus". We repeated the 23rd Psalm, and Jean led in singing "There's a Land That is Fairer Than Day". Beatrice led us in praying The Lord's Prayer. I led the singing of "There's A New Name Written Down in Glory", a song I hadn't sung for years and one that is found in few hymnbooks. Instead of the words "and it's mine, O yes, it's mine," referring to the new name written down in heaven, we substituted the words "and it's David's, O yes, it's David's". Then Bernadette suggested that we remain quiet. As we stood around David's bed in reverential silence, six seconds later David's spirit left his body at 6:35 p.m. The prayer we had prayed together two days earlier had been answered. He was now as we had sung, "safe in the arms of Jesus." This most precious of worship services accompanied by the presence of the Holy Trinity, I believe, was then concluded by a response of joy sung by the angels of heaven. Luke 15:10. This glorious bedside worship time inspired by heavenly hosts was God's Holy Confirmation Sign. Jean, the mother who gave him physical birth, sealed his spiritual rebirth with a kiss.

When David died, he was only 43 years old. Like all of God's redeemed children who cross the river of death, he could offer the prayer written by the Danish theologian and philosopher who died at the age of 42:

"Father In Heaven!

Hold not our sins up against us.

But hold us up against our sins,

So that the thought of Thee should not remind

us

Of what we have committed,

But of what Thou didst forgive;

Not how we went astray,

But how Thou didst save us!" Sören Kierkegaard

Samuel Barber included the above prayer in a chorale he wrote. Prior to those words in the chorale were the words of a prayer of Kierkegaard regarding longing. David had longed for release that he might have a better life, and that longing motivated the prayer we offered. With this in mind, it seems appropriate to reflect upon the thought behind the Danish theologian's prayer pertaining to longing:

"Father in Heaven, longing is Thy gift.

But when longing lays hold of us,

Oh, that we might lay hold of the longing!

When it would carry us away, that

We also might give ourselves up!

When Thou art near to summon us, that

We also in prayer might stay near Thee!

When Thou in the longing dost offer us

The highest good, oh, that we might hold it

Fast!"

Soon after David died, I left his bedroom and went outside where in the western sky I beheld the most beautiful sight I have ever seen. The sun pulsated with ultra colors - blue and violet, and infra colors we associate with a sunset - red, orange and yellow hues, even though it was not a sunset. But what really caught my attention was the emerald sheen which cast green flashes over and around the sun. It had to be a rare sight - one which I had never seen before, or since. The undulating colors bathed in the greenish hue throughout I suppose would be called a corona. Drops of water and dust likely made possible the kaleidoscopic phenomenon. What made the scene even more special was the fact that the sun cast a golden glow on the hilly road beyond David's house, and when the path of light reached his driveway, it turned approximately 40 degrees and led across the gravel driveway up to his patio. What kind of refraction of light could account for what I saw?

I beheld with awe and amazement the sight I viewed for only a few moments and then went to the patio door and excitedly summoned Jean and Bernadette to come at once and see what I had been looking at. They were just as moved by the sight as I was and identified the colors and path of light I saw. Right away Bernadette noted the predominance of the green and saw this as a symbolic announcement to us, as if David with his green eyes looked down upon us to inform us that he was now a part of the heavenly host. Only a person close to David who had spent years with the joy of his artistic handiwork would immediately see this as a fitting communication to those David loved. Regardless of how one may explain the phenomenon we saw, this for me was truly a Holy Sign.

On the next day, July 16th, Jean and I returned home. Because of our weariness we did not drive straight through, but stayed overnight in a motel. The next day when we reached home, there were chores awaiting us that needed attention. That night as we were getting ready for bed I noticed a light shining from upstairs which illuminated the stairway. Thinking that I must have left a light on in my study which was upstairs, I started up the stairway to turn it off. Before I reached the top of the stairs, I realized that this light was coming from a source other than a light originating in my study.

As I entered my study, I saw a bright light from the moon shining through a clearing in the woods behind our home making possible the flooding of my study with light as it entered the room through a window. As I looked more closely at the moon, it too was pulsating as the sun was the day when David died. This undoubtedly was another corona; but what amazed me was the intensity of the light. The undulation was like a heartbeat. Never before or since have I seen anything that even slightly resembles what I have described. This was another Holy Sign seen at a time when Jean and I needed a confirmation of God's presence and benign purpose.

Both the sun and moon which I saw pulsated like the beat of a heart which makes life possible. David's new life in Christ, it seemed, was celebrated by undulations of light. This brings to mind the words of David, the Psalmist, in Psalm 27:1a, "The Lord is my light and my salvation." Knowing the truth of this reality, the Psalmist concludes that there is no reason to fear.

Chapter 12

Looking At The Beauty of God's Presence

Earlier I recorded G. W. Bromiley's comments on the doctrine of providence. In the light of my experience of God's presence during the time of David's ordeal, it is with humble and grateful joy that I view providence as a divine gift described beautifully and succinctly by Bromiley who wrote, "Providence is the preservation, superintendence, and teleological direction of all things by God." p.1020, Volume 3, The International Standard Bible Encyclopedia.

My description in this book of God's providence focuses more on nature than history. My intention is not to exclude history in my description of the way God providentially works, even though history is also the story of human decisions some of which, like the holocaust, result in unimaginable evil. This challenges the contention that somehow even evil, while not congruent with divine purpose, does ultimately serve God's purpose. Even so, I unequivocally believe providence includes the constant outworking in all levels of life of God's all wise and trustworthy purposes. This is made possible by His creative presence in the natural world. In the natural world appropriate resources are provided through the transcendent, immanence of divine sovereign love by which human fulfillment becomes a possibility even in the midst of tragedy when life appears utterly absurd. This truth applies to both nature and history, and to both individual and collective life.

David, the Psalmist, after whom my son was named, wrote in Psalm 19, "The heavens declare the glory of God; the skies proclaim the work of his hands. Day after day they pour forth speech; night after night they display knowledge. There is no speech or language where their voice is not heard. Their voice goes out into all the earth, their words to the end of the world." Verses 1-4. The natural world reveals God to those who have ears to hear and eyes to see.

The link between heaven and earth, that "voice heard" is personified in God-man, Jesus Christ. Paul wrote to Christians in Colosse, who it appears were confronted with the Gnostic Heresy that made Jesus lesser than God: "He is the image of the invisible God, the firstborn over all creation. For by him all things were created: things in heaven and on earth, visible and invisible, whether thrones or powers or rulers or authorities; all things were created by him and for him. he is before all things and in him all things hold together." Colossians 1:15-17.

The Greek scholar M. R. Vincent in his "Word Studies in the New Testament", volume 2, p. 897, has given some helpful comments regarding the nature, revelation, and work of Jesus, the Christ, as set forth in the Colossians passage cited. Concerning "image" he wrote, "Image is more than likeness which may be superficial and incidental. It implies prototype, and embodies the central verity of its prototype." Concerning "first-born", he wrote, "As image points to revelation, so first-born points to eternal preexistence." The New English Bible translates Colossians 1:15: "He is...the primacy over all created things." Concerning the prepositional phrase "in Him" Vincent wrote, "In Him, within the sphere of His personality, reside the creative will and the creative energy, and in that sphere the creative act takes place."

I cite the above comments of Vincent because I believe they help clarify the nature of and the role of God's Son in the creation and maintenance of the universe. In the Colossian passage, I see Jesus, "the image of the invisible God," as the one through whom God's voice is heard in the natural world, and also, the one in whom God's purposes and creative energies are seen, known, and experienced by those who seek to know His Word and will. It is this reality which serves as a basis for Paul's admonition in Philippians 4:8, "Finally, brothers, whatever is true, whatever is noble, whatever is right, whatever is pure, whatever is lovely, whatever is admirable-if anything is excellent or praiseworthy, think about such things." With this in mind, I shall conclude this story of David's life which has focused on his human and spiritual journey, and the positive influence of his life with a description of what I saw as evidence of the beauty of God's presence at his Memorial Service held at St. William's Catholic Church on July 23, 1997, at 6:30 p.m.

David's Memorial Service included moments of festal joy as we celebrated the power, grace and love of God which brought David peace and joy. Even through our tears, we understood the meaning of Frederick William Faber's words when he wrote that God's love is "broader than the measure of man's mind."

In our worship of the God who commanded light to shine out of the darkness, Genesis 1:2-3, God's Spirit opens to us eternal truths reflected in the changing and variegated scenes in the sky above, in the earth below, and in surrounding waters. When we worship in the context of the believing community of faith, varieties of music and other forms of art are often a way of celebrating life as we relate to God, the Giver of all good. The corporate worship of God may occur both through the use of traditional liturgies, and within the context of contemporary settings which dispense with the usual rituals that utilize familiar prayers, scripture and music.

When family members planned David's service, it seemed most fitting to include music he enjoyed over the last three decades of his life. During that time, he was neither a church member or attender. While he was somewhat familiar with church rituals and hymns in his school days, it seemed more appropriate to celebrate life with the use of some of his favorite secular music that in some sense had spiritual meaning for him. So interspersed with a brief homily by Fr. Jerry Stern; a eulogy written by me and read by John; Bernadette's letter dedicated to David and played on tape; David's letter to Bernadette read by Linda; and personal remarks by attendees; nine musical selections were played beginning with an Introduction Tape consisting of BB King's jazz. The other eight selections were played in this order: Annie's Song, Sounds of Silence, Perfect Day, Father and Son by Cat Stevens, Wind Beneath My Wings, Lady in Red, Time in a Bottle, concluding with the Hallelujah Chorus sung while everyone stood. The Hallelujah Chorus was for me, and I am sure for many others attending, a fitting way to celebrate the joyous home-going of David.

Fr. Stern's homily celebrated David's St. Francis-like love of nature. Fittingly, Bernadette's recorded letter to David was a combination paean and lament. David's letter to Bernadette was a deep expression of a love that would not cease. David's thespian friend's comments were an expression of admiration for a very special person. My final words celebrated the fact that David, who loved nature, came to know not only the God of nature, but also the God of redemption in Jesus Christ. As a final word, the preacher in me said that Socrates' dictum, "Know thyself" is realized as one comes to know God, the highest Good who enables us to be happy and useful. The altar girl who participated in the Memorial Service of Celebration and Worship said that though she did not know David, she felt blessed being present for the memorial celebration. She had also spoken eloquently for us who did know him.

Not only was the beauty of God's presence experienced in what we heard, but was wonderfully celebrated by the visual, especially as seen in David's paintings which graced the chancel area. I believe that for many who filled St. William's Church that day these were gifts from David, God's sign maker, sign giver, and artist. A fitting name for what we saw might be "Seasons of The Soul".

In front of the chancel in a central position was the baptismal font on the top of which was a picture of David proudly holding his pet python draped over his left shoulder. The serpent whose neck is held in David's left hand appears to be looking at the viewer. The left side of David's face is visible and his eyes seem to be looking right at the viewer regardless of where the person may be in the interior area of the church facing the chancel.

It seemed fitting to me that the serpent which is a symbol of the fall of humankind in keeping with the Genesis account, and which later became a means of healing as we read in Numbers 21:8-9, should be included in a

84

picture with David on a baptismal font which was in line with a crucifix on the wall in back of the chancel. This symbolism of sacrificial cleansing and healing all associated with David's salvation is powerfully pictured in the words of John's Gospel in chapter 3, and verses 14 and 15 which reads, "And as Moses lifted up the serpent in the wilderness, so must the Son of Man be lifted up, that whoever believes in him may have eternal life."

To the onlooker's right of David's picture in the panorama of "Seasons of the Soul" were painted depictions of the kind of human love that gives life and sustenance to the soul. The music of life begins with birth. Just off the edge of the raised area of the chancel, leaning against the church organ, was David's painting of a dark skinned, smiling mother holding her much loved and contented child. Between David's picture and the painting just described was the portrait of soul mate, Bernadette, placed on the chancel rising and against the background of an array of beautiful flowers. She is wearing sun glasses and her head is saucily tilted.

To the onlooker's extreme left in front of some music stands was David's self-portrait leaning against a music stand situated between two mikes. These objects, which remind me of the music of the soul that gives expression to our emotional nuances in keeping with our changing moods, were on the same level with us congregants. David's self-portrait reveals a person which even friends rarely saw. One sees a contemplative person who is ruminating as if he is wondering, "What's going on here, anyway?" To underscore this thought process that is occurring his chin rests in the palm of his right hand, and the fingers of his hand cover one half of his face below his right eye. Also, the observer sees a large scar beneath the wrist of his right hand. The fact that David wants the viewer to see his scar reveals another aspect of his character many did see. He is saying, "Hey, this is a part of me. I'm not giving up. I'll press on and be who I am even if I don't know all the answers to life." This resolve is reinforced by his eyes that are wide open and by his lips held tightly together. The viewer will also note that the right side of David's face is like his hand and wrist - slightly shadowed. This shadow contrast vis-a-vis the left side of his face speaks to me of the paradoxical dichotomies of life. This self-portrait was indeed the David I saw, loved, served, comforted, and communicated with the last two weeks of his life. Was the David I saw in his self-portrait a harbinger of what would occur the fateful year, 1997?

The story of David's scar is the story of his life. It announced that his laudable epithet was "David, The Determined." How did he get his scar? He was carrying in a canvas holder a glass that he was to install as a replacement for a broken window. The strap broke. The glass shattered and cut a gaping wound in his right arm above his wrist. Immediate attention to his wound insured his survival, but there was a question as to whether he would lose the use of his right hand which was vitally important to the work he did. A lawyer friend of his was fairly certain that he could gain for him a large sum of compensation due to the apparent defect of the carrying case. Furthermore, the lawyer was willing to represent him at no cost. David had no animosity toward the man for whom he was working. In fact, he liked him. Even so, the charge of negligence under the circumstances didn't seem totally unreasonable. In a letter I wrote David, dated May 4, 1985, I urged him to give careful consideration to his options. Despite his plight, I told him that mercy in the situation might be considered to be preferable to pressing for what could be deemed as a just compensation. I told David that regardless of the validity of my advice, I believed I needed to share my thought because it might stimulate "spiritual adrenaline which we all need at times." David took my advice and did not pursue the possibility of a sizable legal compensation. Healing was complete. Even his arm wrestling ability was not impeded.

The next painting to the onlooker's right of David's self-portrait, one which leaned against the end of the altar, was that of an old man. Though likely not intended, it could represent the soul of David had he lived to be a person of mature years. The bright eyes, whimsical smile, and large ears bespeak a character after the mold of David. He seems about to say, "I've got a story to tell you, you won't believe." One can not look at that painting without smiling. That's why I see it as a reflection of David's soul.

Leaning against the other end of the altar was my favorite painting in the panorama of art I have entitled "Seasons of the Soul". A unicorn, a small mythical animal with a single horn in the center of its forehead, is sitting with its legs folded under it on a teal blue rectangular piece of material a few inches thick. To the right of it is a naked man sitting on the same teal blue raised area, with his legs crossed and his right arm draped around the neck and across the body of the animal. The figures are white. They sit partially on an off-white cloth material with folds in it. The cloth covers the middle of the raised area. Green palm fronds are in the background to the right and left of the figures, and other fronds surround an off-white circle behind the man and animal who partially obscure the circle. In the center of the circle one sees more palm fronds. The palm fronds are decorative and give a spiritual quality to the composition. The man's face is simply white with no facial features. Against the background of the picture I have described is blackness.

If I were to give a title to the painting I have described, I would call it "Paradise". Though small, the unicorn was fierce and swift. Legend has it that since the hunter could not capture the animal by normal means, they employed trickery. They would lead a virgin to the spot frequented by the unicorn and leave her there alone. Sensing the purity of the virgin, the unicorn would run to her, lay its head in her lap, and fall asleep. The hunter then effected the capture. The unicorn itself was early accepted by Christianity as a symbol of purity. Thus, Christian writers interpreted the legend of the unicorn and virgin as an allegory of the Annunciation and the Incarnation of Christ, born of a Virgin.

The theme of oneness is pronounced in the painting as seen in the white figure leaning on the unicorn with the off-white circle behind them, and both of them partially sitting on the off-white cloth. It is purity represented by the use of white that makes them one.

Does the faceless man represent those members of the human race who have been made pure because of the sacrifice of the incarnate, sinless Son of God represented by the unicorn? That, indeed, would seem to be an appropriate interpretation of the painting. The palm fronds for Christians have traditionally been symbols of victory, in keeping with the triumphant entry of Jesus into Jerusalem. In the setting of the painting, they would seem to represent a celebration of the triumph of Jesus over sin, death and hell which opened for all believers the doors of Paradise.

Fittingly, now the face of David could be painted on the head of the faceless man. Cleansed of sin by the sacrifice of Jesus, he entered triumphantly into the eternal Kingdom of the Lord. He now experiences a oneness with the Father and Son in answer to Jesus' prayer, John 17:21.

Artist and engraver, Barry Moser whose artistic work may be seen in The Pennyroyal Caxton Bible said, "Religion and art seek to make some order out of chaos." David's paintings which in themselves are a memorial to his life, talent, thought and spiritual depth have met the criterion. They reflect the beauty of God's presence.

Someone may ask, "But on what basis did I presume to interpret the meaning of David's paintings when as far as known, he did not set out to paint what I described?" That is a fair question. My answer relates to what earlier I described as the providence of God which is a phrase that says God in ways often unknown to us provides a spiritual superintendence and sustenance of endeavors which may be discerned by those to whom His Spirit makes the Divine presence known. Reynolds Price in his book, Letter To A Man In The Fire, which was inspired by a young man who was dying with cancer, wrote concerning certain paintings in which he saw suggestions of "immanent or hovering intelligent presence beyond the painter's hand and eye." That I believe I saw in the paintings seen in the chancel area at David's Memorial Service. In them I saw the beauty of God's presence.

Following the Memorial Service as I was standing outside the church, a gentleman came up to me and told me that he was the man for whom David worked when David's arm was cut. He then said to me that when he heard of my son's death and the service to be held at St. William's

Church, he determined he would attend the Memorial Service of "one of the finest persons I ever met." What a glorious, spontaneous, sweet-scented memorial to David these words were. The words come alive as I look at David's picture with the pet serpent which hangs on our bedroom wall. I think of them many other times as well. For me, the words are "spiritual adrenaline".

The beauty of David's life is remembered whenever Jean and I look at the loving man and woman statuette David gave us, and at the urn containing some of David's ashes. Both of these artistic symbols of love are on our fireplace mantel. The urn, a welcomed gift from Bernadette, is a smaller replica of the one placed in front of David's picture at the Memorial Service. It is painted with the prominent colors we saw in the sun's corona after David's death.

Though this book is a testament of our faith in a God whose presence has touched our lives with beauty in a wonderful way through the personalities of our sons, David and John, and daughter, Linda, sometimes we still cry when we realize that David is no longer a phone call away. But Jean and I cry, so to speak, in the arms of the God we know in Jesus, a Man for Others, and who as Immanuel, God with us, cries with us, even as He wept with others when Lazarus died, John 11:33-35. God's love assures us of the certainty that God will continue to be with us, no matter what.

Dear reader, this same loving Lord is always present for you as well. The beauty of God's presence will always be with you. Hear the promise: "God has said, 'Never will I leave you, never will I forsake you'". Hebrews 13:5b.

One way that the beauty of God's presence may be experienced is through a memorial. The giving of a fitting remembrance will help one to slowly move on in the grief process and possibly make the loss a gain for others. Thus the memorial, itself, may be evidence of "The Beauty of God's Presence."

As a memorial to David, Jean and I chose to initiate some money raising events for the benefit of the American Cancer Society. Also, we see the writing of this book, a memorial project which in a real sense has been a collaborative one for Jean and myself, as a means of helping others find God's presence, power and love to be a source of enablement in dealing with losses in their lives. While God's enabling grace will likely work in different ways for others, depending upon their individual needs, His promise will not fail them, or anyone who seeks the Almighty One's comfort and strength.

For the blessing of having David as a son, Jean and I are grateful to our Awesome God, who loves us in the Son of God and Son of Man, Jesus, the Christ; and who created and redeemed a creation that had been lost in chaos and the darkness of sin's blight. In particular, through the difficult days of searching, during a time of great emotional, spiritual and physical testing, we are grateful for the all-sufficient power of God's enabling love and grace which David experienced.

In this written saga of David our chief purpose has been to glorify the God whom we know in Jesus Christ. To the seeker after truth this God gives grace and peace. Among recipients of grace and peace was our son, David Lane Phillips. Though flawed like all mortals, we believe he too is deserving of the tribute which marks the conclusion of Shakespeare's, "Julius Caesar":

"His life was gentle; and the elements

So mix'd in him, that Nature might

stand up and say to the world, 'This

was a man!'"

In retrospect, David may now say in the spirit of Job 23:10: "God knew the way that I took; when he tested me, I came forth as gold."

What David became by God's grace was the personification of the "greater purpose" which he sought and found in Jesus Christ through cancer's "seeming madness."

Epilogue

Lament, The Seedbed of Hope

The first issue of "Time" magazine in the year 2001 showed a picture of Pope John Paul II standing before the Wailing Wall in Jerusalem. What was unusual about the picture was that he stood there in isolation, no doubt for security. Being alone served to emphasize that the Bishop of Rome represented countless millions whose prayer is for peace. Perhaps his prayer also expressed sorrow for the sins of the Church in the midst of a lost world. A prayer of lamentation would seem fitting for one of his station standing as a leader of the Church before the Western Wall, popularly referred to as the Wailing Wall.

To lament or wail is to pray from one's inner being. The prayer of lament without words offers release for the anguish of one's soul. It may be a reflection of a compassionate God who in Jesus Christ wept over Jerusalem before He laid down His life for the sin of humankind on a cross outside the city walls.

The Holy Spirit gives to the believer the power to lament; for we read in Romans 8:26,27, "... the Spirit helps us in our weakness. We do not know what we ought to pray, but the Spirit himself intercedes for us with groans that words cannot express. And he who searches our hearts knows the mind of the Spirit, because the Spirit intercedes for the saints in accordance with God's will." Is it not amazing that God orchestrates our crying during times of bereavement and powerlessness: so that out of our broken-heartedness, hurts and pain we find empowerment, encouragement and strength to go on?

The ability to lament at the time of the loss of a loved one; the death of a relationship during a divorce; or physical and emotional distancing, when losing a job, or having a dream dashed by uncontrollable circumstances can spell salvation when nothing but uncertainty and devastating loss knocks down all the supports we have known in the past.

"Salvation," you say? Yes, for when we have nothing left with which to do battle, a God who cries for us is present. If you have not experienced this kind of succor, perhaps you have sensed that it must be available for more than 40 Psalms in the Old Testament deal with issues of personal sickness, death, persecution, exile, shame and abuse. One whole Old Testament book, Lamentations, is about impassioned grief. Yet, in that same book we read, "Because of the Lord's great love, we are not consumed, for his compassions never fail. They are new every morning; great is your faithfulness. I say to myself, 'The Lord is my portion; therefore I will wait for him.' The Lord is good to those whose hope is in him, to the one who seeks him, it is good to wait quietly for the salvation of the Lord." Lamentations 3:22-26.

In our time of need, we must meet God at our wailing wall. Remember, there is no other way that leads to final salvation, except to be willing to walk the path of adversity and self abandonment. We read in Romans 6:8, "Now if we died with Christ, we believe that we will also live with Him." This truth is illustrated by what we read in Acts 14. Paul and Barnabas refused to be honored as gods. Rather, they welcomed suffering as a gift from God. After being stoned by Jews who came from

Antioch and Iconium, Paul was left for dead. But later he got up and with Barnabas went to Derbe where they preached good news resulting in the winning of many disciples. After that, Paul and Barnabas strengthened the new followers of Jesus and encouraged them "to remain true to the faith;" for they said, "We must go through many hardships to enter the kingdom of God." Acts 14:22.

What is there about adversity and self-abandonment that results in salvation by making it possible for us to enter the kingdom of God? It is the element of lament that is present. Lament allows the full power of reality to engulf us as we address the One who knows so well the implications of what we are facing; and what we are doing, or not doing. The Old Testament prophet, Jeremiah, experienced the wrenching depths of despair when he gave himself over to lament as he heard and felt the inner hurt, frustration and disappointment of Israelites who were blind and deaf to the Word of God that the prophet declared. His lament trailed off into inexpressible sorrow at the possibilities of what would happen to those for whom he wept.

What are some of the positive aspects of lamenting related to daily living and our influence in bringing about change? Lament is prayer in its deepest form; for it is a truthful expression of life as it really is for us. As such, it may be a prelude to stave off disaster, or right the wrong. Crying out to God concerning what disturbs us; what is wrong; what threatens us; what breaks our hearts is a healthy and wholesome expression of prayer in any circumstance. Because Babylon is more visible than the New Jerusalem, it is fitting that we ask, "Is God leaving us to wallow in the mess we and others have created, even as we proclaim the Gospel of redemption?" How is there so much injustice and pain in the world? So we cry out, "My God, my God, how long?"

Is our crying to no avail? Not if we are obedient to our calling to be His faithful witnesses. This means we must strongly lament; for apart from deep concern born of the Spirit, we don't have enough passion to oppose the passionate forces of evil in the name of Christ. Lament arouses passion. The forces of evil will not yield to cool, rational, unimpassioned appeal, even when the appeal expresses God's truth. The appeal needs fire - not destructive, but instructive fire; not attacking fire, but supporting fire. The anguish of the world is an affront to the Creator God. Hope is born in full acceptance of and immersion in the anguish, pain and injustice resident all around us, against which we are to struggle as God's stewards. By the power of God's Holy Spirit working in us His kingdom comes.

Lament allows the full arousal of consciousness, all its dismay, and all its zeal. That is passion worthy of addressing all the principalities and demons of such menacing stature which are running amuck among us.

Memory should play an important role in lament. Recall the rhythm in many of the Psalms which help us to face the now as we remember what has been. The cry of forsakeness in Psalm 22, which Jesus quoted on the cross, is an example of lament which leads to the reaffirmation of faith. Interspersed among the woes is remembrance of what God has done in the past. Let our lament include the recovery of memory. Then realizing the full brunt of what is happening now, we are thrown back on what gives us a sense of security, which in turn gives us endurance in the present and hope for the future.

During the Iranian hostage crisis, at the time of President Carter's administration, one of the American hostages remembered many Biblical passages and hymns which were a storehouse of assurance making possible a gateway to recovery of hope. Without a catalog of memory, this would not have been possible.

So even as we lament our state and the conditions of the world that has distanced itself from God, we need to remember that God has not forsaken us. When we truly arouse our passions by feeling pain keenly, then we must not fail to turn to God with it. Knowing something of the pain that Jesus felt when he gave His life that we might have eternal life, and in so doing cried out, "My God, my God, why hast thou forsaken me," let us cry out for peace and freedom from destruction, not only for ourselves, but also for our world. Then we must declare with passion in word and in deed that God through the cross of Jesus has laid claim to a lost world.

As we rise with faith and obedience to new life in Christ, God will come with resurrection power to give hope, even as we lament. Through the resurrection of Jesus Christ we may declare with the psalmist, "For his anger lasts only a moment, but his favor lasts a lifetime; weeping may remain for a night, but rejoicing comes in the morning." Psalm 30:5. So in confidence let us say, "Why are you downcast, O my soul? Why so disturbed within me? Put your hope in God, for I will yet praise him, my Savior and my God." Psalm 42:11

Lloyd Austin Phillips

About The Author

The academic and pastoral background of the author, Lloyd Austin Phillips, helped qualify him to write *Cancer's Seeming Madness*. He earned a Bachelor of Divinity degree from Calvin Seminary in Grand Rapids, MI. At the same institution, he earned a Th.M. with a major in Philosophical Theology. In earning the latter degree, he wrote as his thesis, "Painting, A Vehicle For Christian Apologetics" which dealt with how three master painters working in different eras used their talents to create works which served the purpose of defending the Christian faith by making the faith more palatable and vivid for the average person.

This academic preparation paved the way for forty-one years of ordained ministry in the United Methodist Church. In three of the parishes served, major building projects were pursued to provide adequate facilities for new ministries essential to growing congregations.

In Lansing, Michigan, Reverend Phillips founded the Dismas Counseling Service for ex-convicts and their families. He also wrote scripts for and conducted a weekly TV program called *Cornerstone*. Later in his ministry, he served as President of the Samaritan Counseling Center and was the conference speaker through Michigan State University Extension on the subject of "Ethics in the Public Square."

Most of all, Reverend Phillips' continuous presence with his son, David, during the last two weeks of his life made it possible for him to write, *Cancer's Seeming Madness*, a book possessing academic and pastoral integrity.

Printed in the United States
6138